Contents

Choosing your Coursebook

Alan Cunningsworth

Heinemann English Language Teaching
Halley Court, Jordan Hill, Oxford OX2 8EJ
A division of Reed Educational & Professional Publishing Limited

OXFORD MADRID FLORENCE ATHENS PRAGUE SÃO PAULO
MEXICO CITY CHICAGO PORTMOUTH(NH) TOKYO SINGAPORE
KUALA LUMPUR MELBOURNE AUCKLAND JOHANNESBURG
IBADAN GABORONE

Heinemann is a registered trademark of Reed Educational & Professional Publishing Limited

ISBN 0 435 24058 7

Designed by Giles Davies

Cover photo by Moggy

The authors and publishers would like to thank the following for
permission to reproduce their material:

Cambridge University Press for the extracts on pp 26 (below), 48,
69, 78, 82-3, 89, 100, 121; Heinemann ELT for the extracts on pp
11, 13 (below), 18–19, 21, 22, 24, 26 (above), 39, 40, 47, 49, 52, 74,
77, 79, 81, 87, 94, 95, 105, 107 (above), 108, 123; Longman Group
for the extracts on pp 12 (centre), 29, 35, 36, 37, 45, 51 (below), 76,
104-5, 124, 125, 145, 146, 147; Nelson ELT for the extracts on pp
12 (above), 33; Oxford University Press for the extracts on pp 27
(above), 42, 44, 51 (above), 107 (below), 119, 120, 142–3; Penerbit
Fajar Bakti for the extract on p 140; Phoenix ELT for the Macmillan
extracts on pp 12 (below), 13 (above), 27 (below), 65, 66, 71, 72,
122.

Printed and bound in Great Britain by The Bath Press

97 98 99 10 9 8 7 6 5 4 3 2

Preface

This book is a development of an earlier book entitled *Evaluating and Selecting EFL Teaching Materials* and is completely redesigned and rewritten. I hope that it will meet the need encountered by many teachers, course directors, teacher trainers and trainees for an up-to-date book on this important subject, which is both accessible and practical, and addresses the main issues.

Probably nothing influences the content and nature of teaching and learning more than the books and other teaching material used. So it is of great importance that the best and most appropriate materials available should be adopted. Selecting teaching materials is often not an easy task, but I hope that this book will help to make it a little easier, and will help to ensure that the choices made are the best possible ones.

I would like to acknowledge the great debt which I owe to colleagues and to students on training courses over a period of years for their valuable comments and suggestions, which have helped me to develop and refine the evaluation criteria put forward in this book.

Introduction

The aim of this book is to help teachers of English as a foreign or second language to evaluate coursebooks and select those that will be most suitable for their purposes. It will be of equal use to course designers, directors of studies and others who have to make decisions about which coursebooks and other teaching material to adopt.

The book will also be of interest to teacher trainers and to those undertaking training courses for EFL or ESL. A needs-analysis survey of teacher training in TEFL/TESL showed that employing institutions and others with an interest in the content of teacher training courses considered coursebook evaluation to be one of the most important components of a teacher training course (Henrichsen 1983). I hope that this book will provide some theoretical and practical input that will be useful in covering this element of EFL/ESL training.

The contents of the book are intended to be essentially practical in nature. For ease of reference, evaluation criteria are highlighted and directly follow the section that they refer to. In this way, they are immediately accessible to anyone wishing to use them without working through the explanatory text.

However, some underlying principles or guidelines for evaluation are necessary in order to give a rationale to the evaluation criteria that are used. These general guidelines are included in Chapter 2 of the book, and the evaluation criteria in this book are founded on them. Effective evaluation depends on asking appropriate questions and interpreting the answers to them. This book provides a wide range of evaluation questions for you to select from according to your individual situation. There are also a good many pointers on interpreting the sort of information that will emerge, although your choice of coursebook will ultimately depend on your own professional judgement.

A large number of examples have been used, drawn from contemporary British coursebooks and supporting material, which will help to illustrate the points being made and suggest how the evaluation criteria can be applied in practice. The case studies in particular are intended to show how evaluation procedures can be carried out, focusing on different aspects of coursebooks. I should stress here, however, that this book is not intended as a comprehensive review of EFL coursebooks and other teaching materials. Its aim is to help equip teachers and others to do their own evaluation and selection of materials. The fact that an example from a coursebook has been included should not necessarily be taken as an endorsement of that book, nor should the absence of any current coursebook be taken to imply lack of approval.

Chapter 1 Selecting coursebooks – the essentials

The wealth of published material for English language teaching (ELT) available on the market makes selecting the right coursebook a challenging task. We need to be able to make informed and appropriate choices when selecting coursebooks and supporting materials. An ever-increasing number of books are being published across more and more areas of ELT to the point where it is easy to become thoroughly confused and overwhelmed by their sheer variety and by the competing claims made for them. This applies to mainstream courses and also to more specialized material such as ESP courses and supplementary skills books.

Learners are becoming more sophisticated, particularly through the influence of television and computer games, and they expect high standards of production and presentation, especially where visuals are concerned. They also expect textbooks to make learning easier and more enjoyable and can be quick to lose interest in dull and uninspiring material, no matter how sound it may be methodologically. Faced with the rich variety of coursebooks available, how do we make our choices? Should we choose the books with the most attractive illustrations? Would we be best advised to go for the ones that are strongly made and look as though they will survive several years of fairly rough classroom use? Is it advisable to select among the cheapest, leaving more money in the budget for buying equipment such as cassette players?

These are just a few of the factors that need to be taken into account, and not necessarily the most important. As in most decision-making, the key lies in asking the right questions first and then evaluating the answers which result from this process.

1 Approaches to evaluation

We can form a general impression of a coursebook fairly quickly, just by looking through it and getting an overview of its possibilities and its strengths and weaknesses, noting significant features which stand out. This is what most of us would do when sample copies of a new course land on our desk. We can soon see what various features of the coursebook are like, such as the quality of the visuals, how attractive and clear the layout is, what the whole course package is made up of, how the items included in the coursebook are sequenced, etc. This kind of **impressionistic overview** is useful and gives us a general introduction to the material. It is particularly appropriate when doing a preliminary sift through a lot of coursebooks before making a shortlist for more detailed analysis, and also when looking at new material that may be considered for adoption at a later date. But it will not necessarily identify any significant omissions in the coursebook or locate any important weaknesses. Nor can it be relied on to give enough detail to ensure a good match between what the coursebook contains and the requirements of the learning/teaching situation.

For this we need **in-depth evaluation** which is more penetrating in its approach and has its own agenda. As well as seeing what is prominent and obvious in a coursebook, we need to examine how specific items are dealt with, particularly those which relate to students' learning needs, syllabus requirements, how different aspects of language are dealt with, etc.

Many of us will have our individual checklist of things that we look at in a new coursebook. How the book deals with these items will give us a good indication of how suitable it would be. Some of my favourite questions in this context are:

- How does the coursebook present the present perfect, with particular reference to its meaning and use?
- How does it teach the use of articles?
- Does it include anything on intonation?
- Does it deal with the organization of language above the level of the sentence, eg in conversation or in continuous writing?

These are all areas which tend to tax coursebook writers because they are difficult for most learners and are not very easy to teach. There are many other key indicators of this kind that you could use, depending on your own learners and their backgrounds. You may like to consider here which indicators you think would be most useful for you. They need not be limited to aspects of language, but could include topic, approach to learning, organization of content, teaching techniques employed, and many others.

It is also useful to pick out one or two units of a coursebook and analyse them in detail, trying to choose units which look as though they are typical of the material as a whole. Here you could look at the balance of activities and skills contained in a unit, the potential for learner participation, the amount of new language introduced, the amount of recycling, etc. Again, which aspects of the material you examine will depend on your priorities and on the characteristics of the students that you are working with and the context that you are working in.

The in-depth approach is characterized by its active nature: we actively seek out information about the material in line with an agenda that we have already decided on. The impressionistic approach is more receptive in that we look for anything that is noteworthy and interesting.

A combination of both approaches, involving an impressionistic overview of the whole and an in-depth examination of representative samples of the material will form a sound basis for evaluation and for the ensuing choice of the most suitable coursebook for adoption.

2   Deciding on a checklist

There are many criteria that can be used for evaluating coursebooks and I will be discussing many of them in later chapters of this book. However, for practical purposes a manageable list of the most important criteria will be needed. As different criteria will apply in different circumstances, it is best to identify your own priorities and draw up your own checklist, perhaps using some of the criteria outlined in this book and adding others of your own, based on your concerns and priorities. As a starting point, I have selected what seem to me to be some of the most important general criteria for evaluation and selection purposes and present them here as a basic quick-reference checklist.

Quick-reference checklist for evaluation and selection

Aims and approaches

☐ Do the aims of the coursebook correspond closely with the aims of the teaching programme and with the needs of the learners?

☐ Is the coursebook suited to the learning/teaching situation?

☐ How comprehensive is the coursebook? Does it cover most or all of what is needed? Is it a good resource for students and teachers?

☐ Is the coursebook flexible? Does it allow different teaching and learning styles?

Design and organization

☐ What components make up the total course package (eg students' books, teachers' books, workbooks, cassettes, etc)?

☐ How is the content organized (eg according to structures, functions, topics, skills, etc)? Is the organization right for learners and teachers?

☐ How is the content sequenced (eg on the basis of complexity, 'learnability', usefulness, etc)?

☐ Is the grading and progression suitable for the learners? Does it allow them to complete the work needed to meet any external syllabus requirements?

☐ Is there adequate recycling and revision?

☐ Are there reference sections for grammar, etc? Is some of the material suitable for individual study?

☐ Is it easy to find your way around the coursebook? Is the layout clear?

Language content

☐ Does the coursebook cover the main grammar items appropriate to each level, taking learners' needs into account?

☐ Is material for vocabulary teaching adequate in terms of quantity and range of vocabulary, emphasis placed on vocabulary development, strategies for individual learning?

☐ Does the coursebook include material for pronunciation work? If so what is covered: individual sounds, word stress, sentence stress, intonation?

☐ Does the coursebook deal with the structuring and conventions of language use above sentence level, eg how to take part in conversations, how to structure a piece of extended writing, how to identify the main points in a reading passage? (More relevant at intermediate and advanced levels.)

☐ Are style and appropriacy dealt with? If so, is language style matched to social situation?

Skills

☐ Are all four skills adequately covered, bearing in mind your course aims and syllabus requirements?

☐ Is there material for integrated skills work?

☐ Are reading passages and associated activities suitable for your students' levels, interests, etc? Is there sufficient reading material?

☐ Is listening material well recorded, as authentic as possible, accompanied by background information, questions and activities which help comprehension?

☐ Is material for spoken English (dialogues, roleplays, etc) well designed to equip learners for real-life interactions?

☐ Are writing activities suitable in terms of amount of guidance/control, degree of accuracy, organization of longer pieces of writing (eg paragraphing) and use of appropriate styles?

Topic

☐ Is there sufficient material of genuine interest to learners?

☐ Is there enough variety and range of topic?

☐ Will the topics help expand students' awareness and enrich their experience?

☐ Are the topics sophisticated enough in content, yet within the learners' language level?

☐ Will your students be able to relate to the social and cultural contexts presented in the coursebook?

☐ Are women portrayed and represented equally with men?

☐ Are other groups represented, with reference to ethnic origin, occupation, disability, etc?

Methodology

☐ What approach/approaches to language learning are taken by the coursebook? Is this appropriate to the learning/teaching situation?

☐ What level of active learner involvement can be expected? Does this match your students' learning styles and expectations?

☐ What techniques are used for presenting/practising new language items? Are they suitable for your learners?

☐ How are the different skills taught?

☐ How are communicative abilities developed?

☐ Does the material include any advice/help to students on study skills and learning strategies?

☐ Are students expected to take a degree of responsibility for their own learning (eg by setting their own individual learning targets)?

Teachers' books

☐ Is there adequate guidance for the teachers who will be using the coursebook and its supporting materials?

☐ Are the teachers' books comprehensive and supportive?

☐ Do they adequately cover teaching techniques, language items such as grammar rules and culture-specific information?

☐ Do the writers set out and justify the basic premises and principles underlying the material?

☐ Are keys to exercises given?

Practical considerations

☐ What does the whole package cost? Does this represent good value for money?

☐ Are the books strong and long-lasting? Are they attractive in appearance?

☐ Are they easy to obtain? Can further supplies be obtained at short notice?

☐ Do any parts of the package require particular equipment, such as a language laboratory, listening centre or video player? If so, do you have the equipment available for use and is it reliable?

3 Selecting the best available coursebook

Selecting coursebooks involves matching the material against the context in which it is going to be used. No coursebook designed for a general market will be absolutely ideal for your particular group of learners, but the aim is to find the best possible fit, together with potential for adapting or supplementing parts of the material where it is inadequate or unsuitable.

A sound way to approach the selection of coursebooks is firstly to identify the aims and objectives of your teaching programme and secondly to analyse the learning/teaching situation in which the material will be used. This will give you a profile of the context for which you are selecting the teaching materials and some of the requirements that the materials will have to meet.

The next stage is to draw up a list of potential coursebooks, using information from publishers, advice from colleagues and your own previous experience. These books should be subjected to an impressionistic evaluation to eliminate those that are obviously unsuitable. The resulting shortlist should consist of perhaps between three and five coursebooks and these will be the subject of an in-depth evaluation process using criteria which are most relevant to the needs of the teachers and learners concerned. These criteria can be selected from among those presented in this book or devised specially to meet specific needs and circumstances. In most cases there will be a combination of ready-made and specially-devised criteria.

Materials evaluation is a complex matter, as there are many variables that affect the success or failure of coursebooks when they are in use. The number of variables is reflected in the range and multiplicity of possible evaluation criteria. However, it is important to limit the number of criteria used, the number of questions asked, to manageable proportions. Otherwise we risk being swamped in a sea of detail. This is why it is important to prioritize the criteria that you are going to use, using those which are most relevant to the context in which the materials will be used. The selection of appropriate criteria is crucial, as the evaluation process will throw up a profile of the coursebooks being examined. This profile should then be matched against the profile of the learning/teaching context and of the requirements that have to be met. In most circumstances, the coursebook which most closely fits the requirements and the context will be the best available, although other factors, such as flexibility and the potential for adaptation, will need to be taken into account.

I do not wish to give the impression that the selection process is in any way automatic, as it is not. Nor is it wholly objective, as individual, subjective judgements of a professional nature are central to it. My aim in outlining a procedure for selection is to enhance the value of professional judgement by providing a framework in which it can operate. Also, it is intended as a framework, not a straitjacket, and you will probably want to modify any procedures to suit your circumstances and preferred way of working.

Whatever procedures you do follow, you would be well advised to view materials selection as a process involving several people working together and pooling their perceptions and experience. In this way there is a better chance of making balanced judgements and ultimately of making the best choice of coursebook.

4   Specifying aims and analysing the learning/teaching situation

This is a shortened version of a more comprehensive checklist, which will be found in the Appendix. It should act as a starting point for looking at the context in which teaching materials will be evaluated.

Aims and objectives

- ☐ What are the aims of the English programme?
- ☐ Note any specific objectives, eg in terms of language items, functions, skills to be covered.
- ☐ Is there a detailed syllabus? If so, what does it consist of and how is it organized (in terms of grammar, functions, topics, skills, etc)?
- ☐ How is the achievement of aims and objectives measured?

The learning/teaching situation

- ☐ What is the status and role of English in the learners' home countries?
- ☐ What are their main reasons for learning English?
- ☐ How much time is available? How intensive is the programme?
- ☐ What is the class size? Are classes homogeneous with respect to age, level, ability, etc of the learners?
- ☐ What resources are available including teaching rooms, equipment, supplementary materials, access to photocopying?

The learners

- ☐ What are their ages, levels, expectations, motivation?
- ☐ What is their previous language-learning experience?
- ☐ What are their preferred learning styles?
- ☐ What are their interests?

The teachers

- ☐ What is the accepted role of teachers in the educational system?
- ☐ What methodological approach do they tend to prefer?
- ☐ What level of personal initiative do they bring to their teaching?
- ☐ How free are they to diverge from the syllabus?
- ☐ Do they have the right to adapt or supplement the standard coursebook? If they do, do they have the time and expertise to do so when necessary?

5 The role of coursebooks

Coursebooks are best seen as a resource in achieving aims and objectives that have already been set in terms of learner needs. They should not determine the aims themselves or *become* the aims. We are primarily concerned with teaching the language and not the textbook. When we occasionally talk about 'teaching Unit 16', 'doing the first six chapters' or 'reaching page 68', it is to be hoped that we are only using a convenient shorthand way of expressing well-thought-out aims and objectives and that the coursebook has not become the main determiner of them.

Coursebooks have multiple roles in ELT and can serve as:

- a resource for presentation material (spoken and written)
- a source of activities for learner practice and communicative interaction
- a reference source for learners on grammar, vocabulary, pronunciation, etc
- a source of stimulation and ideas for classroom language activities
- a syllabus (where they reflect learning objectives which have already been determined)
- a resource for self-directed learning or self-access work
- a support for less experienced teachers who have yet to gain in confidence.

It is generally accepted that the role of the coursebook is to be at the service of teachers and learners but not to be their master. Its role is not to exercise a tyrannical function as the arbiter of course content and teaching methods. However, it has to be recognized that teaching materials can exert considerable influence over what teachers teach and how they do it. Consequently, it is of crucial importance that careful selection is made and that the materials selected closely reflect the aims, methods and values of the teaching programme.

The relationship between teacher and coursebook is an important consideration and is at its best when it is a partnership which shares common goals to which each side brings its special contribution. The aims of the coursebook should correspond as closely as possible to the aims of the teacher, and both should seek to meet the needs of the learners to the highest degree. The partnership is helped when aims and objectives are well defined, and when the different but complementary roles of teacher and coursebook are clearly perceived and well balanced.

Chapter 2 Analysing and evaluating coursebooks: a rationale and some guidelines

Selecting coursebooks can involve major strategic decisions, such as when choosing the main course for a five-year teaching programme. Large sums of money are going to be invested over a period of years, and, even more importantly, the learning experiences and eventual level of proficiency in English of large numbers of students will be affected, with possible implications for their future careers. Having once embarked on the introduction of a new integrated course, with students' books, teachers' books, workbooks, cassettes and possibly other components such as pronunciation books and readers, it is very difficult to extricate yourself if a wrong decision has been made. Decisions to use a particular course which are made in one year can have implications for purchasing and using more advanced levels of the same course in subsequent years. Once students have embarked on a particular route to learning using a range of integrated course materials, it can be very difficult to change direction later within the same programme.

1 Selecting coursebooks

In circumstances like these it is absolutely crucial to be confident that the course materials selected are the best and most appropriate available. One way towards this goal is to try out or pilot new material before adopting it. Ideally a number of competing courses could be piloted for a couple of years and the results compared. In reality, there are too many courses available for them all to be tried out, and in most cases piloting, valuable though it is, will be restricted for purely practical reasons to using a small range of material for a relatively short length of time. Nonetheless, information and opinions gained from this kind of trial use can be of great value and new courses should always be tried out before wholesale adoption, wherever possible.

Another approach is to seek the opinions of practising teachers both within and outside your own institution. This is particularly valuable when others have already had some experience of using the materials in question. In time a general consensus tends to develop among schools with similar types of students about which courses are particularly well suited to their needs.

Students' views on the usefulness of coursebooks are also worth canvassing. They may not be as articulate in the language of ELT as their teachers, but very often they know which books they like and which they don't like. Some students can go further than this and give very cogent reasons for their preferences. After all, they are the prime users of the material and with some prompting and carefully chosen questions they can provide very useful feedback.

Where there is no opportunity to talk to people who have actually used the material, and where piloting is not feasible, as, for example, when setting up a completely new teaching programme, then a detailed analysis of the material is the best way of becoming familiar with it. Indeed the same procedure is also invaluable in supplementing information and opinions that have been obtained from others.

This detailed analysis is at the core of the evaluation process and, if carried out as comprehensively as possible, will throw up a good deal of information about the course material under scrutiny. It is possible to analyse several similar courses within a relatively short period of time and to compare the results. Supplemented by experience gained from trying out parts of the material, and views obtained from any colleagues and students who have used it, the results of a detailed analysis provide the basis of successful evaluation and selection.

Analysis is more or less neutral, seeking information in a range of categories, and provides the necessary data for the second stage of the process. This is the **interpretation** of the data obtained. Here a good deal of professional judgement and experience comes into play as the implications of the analysis are worked out and issues such as the relative importance of different aspects of the coursebook are taken into account.

The third stage, **evaluation**, necessarily involves value judgements on the part of those involved. Such value judgements will inevitably be subjective to some extent and will reflect the views and priorities of those making them. They will tend to be based on a number of factors, including the following: learner and teacher expectations; methodological preferences; the perceived needs of the learners; syllabus requirements; and personal preferences.

Selection is the fourth stage of this process and involves matching the features identified during the previous stages against the requirements of a particular learning/teaching situation. It is idealistic to expect a perfect fit, as coursebooks are produced for wide markets and cannot completely meet the demands of every individual class, but selecting within the material and adapting and supplementing it where necessary will overcome minor deficiencies. Some ideas on adapting materials are contained in Chapter 12.

Establishing a set of general criteria beforehand to guide the process can be useful as this will set out clearly and explicitly what some of the agreed values are. For instance, one of the criteria might be that a communicative course is more desirable than one with a purely grammatical approach. Another could be that a general course should include a component on pronunciation. Courses, once analysed, could then be evaluated against a set of criteria which had been agreed previously and set out for reference.

2   Uses of coursebooks

In practice, given the widely differing circumstances prevailing in the world of English language teaching, the roles of coursebooks in the learning/teaching process can vary considerably, reflecting the nature of the partnership between the teacher and the coursebook. The amount of reliance placed on the coursebook by the teacher and the extent to which he or she depends on the book is indicative of the perceived place of the coursebook in the whole learning/teaching process. This can also often tell us a lot about the underlying approach of the educational system in question.

In some cases the book will be followed very closely and in the exact order of presentation. Every text will be carefully studied and each exercise meticulously worked through. Such an approach is characteristic of schools in countries where the syllabus is set centrally and where an officially approved coursebook is prescribed for use. A similar situation may occur on short summer courses employing relatively inexperienced and untrained teachers. Here, the best hope of providing effective teaching may be to supply a relatively foolproof course requiring the use of only a limited range of teaching techniques and providing clear straightforward instructions to the teacher. This is arguably an acceptable strategy for coping with a shortage of experienced qualified staff, and much of the responsibility for the quality of the teaching provided is assumed by the coursebook.

Disadvantages of this approach include the following:

- a possible lack of variety in teaching procedures
- a reduced range of response to individual student needs and problems
- a possible lack of spontaneity
- a sharply reduced level of creativity in teaching technique and language use.

Heavy dependence on coursebooks is far from ideal as it reduces the importance of the individual contributions that good teachers make at all levels in the learning process. It can stifle innovation and it severely limits flexibility. There are circumstances, however, where it is the best available option and is therefore justifiably adopted.

A more balanced relationship between teacher and coursebook holds where teachers are able to select material from a range of alternative courses, or where there is one basic coursebook supported by a variety of supplementary materials. In situations such as these, the main coursebook, which will often have been chosen by the teachers themselves, serves as a useful framework for language content and sequencing but is used selectively, and is supplemented by other material whenever this is thought to be desirable.

An approach of this kind has a number of advantages:

- there is a common framework provided by the coursebook
- less experienced teachers can use the coursebook as heavily as they need to
- there is scope for replacing weaker parts of the standard coursebook with other books or using own material
- there is scope for teachers to develop as they become less dependent on the book and gain in confidence to experiment with alternative materials
- more variety of classroom activity and teaching technique is possible
- a more flexible response to individual students' needs is possible.

At the other extreme we may find schools where there is a syllabus but no set coursebook and where teachers, working within the overall syllabus, construct their own lessons and sequences of lessons from a large array of published, in-house and individually produced material. Some may find such freedom and responsibility frightening, whilst others may revel in it. The scope for creativity, flexibility and originality in such circumstances is limited only by teachers' ability, energy and time, but it must be stressed that such an approach, if potentially very rewarding, can be demanding and time-consuming for those involved.

Factors influencing the degree of dependence or autonomy in using coursebooks include these:

- type of educational system/environment
- syllabus/materials constraints imposed by education authorities
- culture and expectations of learners
- nature and amount of training for teachers
- teachers' experience and confidence
- teachers' command of English (if non-native speakers)
- availability of alternative coursebooks and resources for materials production.

3 What the coursebooks claim

Coursebooks vary considerably in their outlook, in their approach to learning and in their content. The following examples, mainly taken from the back covers of coursebooks, illustrate the sort of claims made for published courses, and give an impression of the rich, but potentially confusing variety of approaches, content and methods in ELT materials. As you look through them, ask yourself a few questions about them, such as these:

- Which descriptions attract you most? Why?
- Which claims are you most sceptical about?
- Are there any common features in the publishers' blurbs?
- What features do publishers seem to think will make their courses attractive?
- Do publishers' blurbs influence you? Do you feel that you can rely on them?

Heinemann Integrated Skills

A series of four levels; elementary, intermediate, upper intermediate and advanced. It represents a new approach to skills teaching, in which integrated skills activities bring together reading, writing, listening and speaking in a natural and realistic way, and provide a balanced method for students to practise and develop their language skills.

At each level there is a **Skills Book**, the core of the series, which contains work on reading, writing, listening and speaking; a **Workbook** which provides language support for the topics covered in the Skills Book; and a **Cassette**, which can be used in conjunction with both books.

From *Heinemann Integrated Skills Series* (Heinemann)

Relay 3 is the third level of a four-level course.

Relay is a specially designed course for young learners and teenagers attending summer schools and short courses. **Relay** has been written by teachers experienced at teaching learners in this age range and is based on the views and comments of many teachers working on short courses in recent years.

Relay 3 is for intermediate and late intermediate learners. It is divided into two laps, each containing enough material for 30 to 40 hours of teaching so there is 60-80 hours in total.

Relay encourages:
● language in use   ● communicative English   ● lively student participation and interaction
● confidence in oral/aural skills   ● grammatical competence   ● vocabulary development

From *Relay 3*, Greenow (Nelson 1990)

Blueprint Intermediate is a fully-integrated course for students who have completed two to three years' study of English.

Blueprint answers the specific needs and problems of the intermediate learner in a way that is constantly challenging and highly motivating. It offers material which builds confidence and learner independence, and improves fluency and accuracy in the four skills.

From *Blueprint Intermediate*, Abbs and Freebairn (Longman 1989)

ENGLISH AROUND YOU is a three-level course for people who require material which will take account of their need to use English as a medium of communication in a non-English speaking environment. It takes them from lower to upper intermediate level.

The vast majority of English learners today need to use the language as a means of international communication. Coursebook content which is centred on British life and culture is irrelevant to these needs, and makes it difficult for the student to relate to his/her own communicative requirements.

ENGLISH AROUND YOU recognises this reality, and allows the learner to:
★   use English in relation to his/her own world
★   act as mediator between L1 and L2
★   extend his/her use of English in an international context

From *English Around You*, Potter (Macmillan 1989)

CAMPUS ENGLISH

CAMPUS ENGLISH is a study skills course for students at university and pre-university level, written in collaboration with the Centre for British Teachers.

CAMPUS ENGLISH has a task-based methodology, which encourages the individual student to establish and reinforce study skills in relation to his or her own specialist field of study.

From *Campus English*, Forman *et al* (Macmillan 1990)

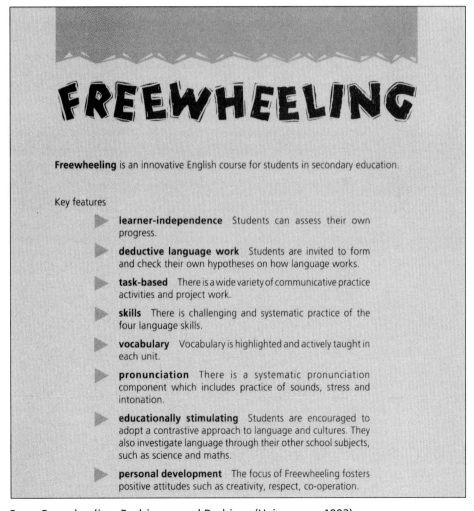

FREEWHEELING

Freewheeling is an innovative English course for students in secondary education.

Key features

▶ **learner-independence** Students can assess their own progress.

▶ **deductive language work** Students are invited to form and check their own hypotheses on how language works.

▶ **task-based** There is a wide variety of communicative practice activities and project work.

▶ **skills** There is challenging and systematic practice of the four language skills.

▶ **vocabulary** Vocabulary is highlighted and actively taught in each unit.

▶ **pronunciation** There is a systematic pronunciation component which includes practice of sounds, stress and intonation.

▶ **educationally stimulating** Students are encouraged to adopt a contrastive approach to language and cultures. They also investigate language through their other school subjects, such as science and maths.

▶ **personal development** The focus of Freewheeling fosters positive attitudes such as creativity, respect, co-operation.

From *Freewheeling*, Rodriguez and Barbisan (Heinemann 1992)

4   Types of materials evaluation

Evaluation can take place before a coursebook is used, during its use and after use, depending on circumstances and the purposes for which the evaluation is being undertaken. Although probably the most common, **pre-use evaluation** is also the most difficult kind of evaluation as there is no actual experience of using the book for us to draw on. In this case we are looking at future or potential performance of the coursebook.

In-use evaluation refers to coursebook evaluation whilst the material is in use, for example when a newly introduced coursebook is being monitored or when a well-established but ageing coursebook is being assessed to see whether it should be considered for replacement.

Post-use evaluation provides retrospective assessment of a coursebook's performance and can be useful for identifying strengths and weaknesses which emerge over a period of continuous use. Evaluation of this kind can be useful in helping to decide whether to use the same coursebook on future occasions, particularly in respect of short self-contained courses which are repeated from time to time.

5   Purposes of materials evaluation

Reasons for materials evaluation activities are many and varied. The intention to adopt new coursebooks is a major and frequent reason for evaluation. Another reason is to identify particular strengths and weaknesses in coursebooks already in use, so that optimum use can be made of their strong points, whilst their weaker areas can be strengthened through adaptation or by substituting material from other books. Inevitably evaluation will involve elements of comparison, especially when coursebooks are in competition for adoption or where existing materials are being challenged by newly produced material. For comparative evaluation of this kind, a standard procedure and a common set of criteria, applied evenly to the different coursebooks, will be of great help in making the process more objective, leading to more reliable results.

Coursebook analysis and evaluation is useful in teacher development and helps teachers to gain good and useful insights into the nature of the material. Similarly, in teacher training, materials evaluation is a valuable component and serves the dual purpose of sensitizing student teachers to some of the more important features to look for in coursebooks and familiarizing them with a range of published materials.

6 Evaluating for potential and evaluating for suitability

In some cases we want to evaluate coursebooks in general, without having particular classes or learners in mind. For example, a new book could be evaluated to see what it might be good for and in what situations it could be expected to be successful. This is evaluation of materials for their **potential,** without any predetermined use in mind. Teacher-training courses often adopt this kind of evaluation for potential so as to equip students with criteria for more specific evaluation at a later date.

Evaluation for **suitability** involves matching the coursebook against a specific requirement including the learners' objectives, the learners' background, the resources available, etc. The basic difference between evaluation for potential and for suitability is highlighted by contrasting the question 'What would this coursebook be good for?' with 'Would it be good for my class?'

7 Guidelines for evaluation

The following guidelines underlie many of the more specific criteria for evaluation which will be found later in this book and act as useful guides in approaching any materials evaluation exercise.

Guideline One

Coursebooks should correspond to learners' needs. They should match the aims and objectives of the language-learning programme.

Aims and objectives can reflect learners' needs in terms of both language content and communicative abilities. Coursebooks should be selected which will help in attaining these objectives. The aims and objectives of a learning/teaching programme should determine which course materials are used, and not vice-versa, reflecting the principle that coursebooks are better servants than masters. It is very important that coursebooks should facilitate learners' progress and take them forward as effectively as possible towards their goals. Consequently the content of the material should correspond to what students need to learn, in terms of language items, skills and communicative strategies.

Guideline Two

Coursebooks should reflect the uses (present or future) which learners will make of the language. Select coursebooks which will help to equip students to use language effectively for their own purposes.

The learning/teaching programme should have at its base a clear view of what students need to learn in order to make effective use of the language in personal, professional, academic or whatever other situations are relevant. The most suitable coursebooks for your learners will reflect as closely as possible the language content, language skills and patterns of language use that are needed. This involves us in looking beyond the confines of the classroom and focusing our attention on the use which individual learners will make of what they have learned.

There is a definite place in a learning/teaching programme for grammar exercises, dialogue work and all the other procedures which contribute to the learning process. Indeed, that place may very often be a large one. But we should also remember that such activities and teaching techniques are a means to an end and not an end in themselves.

Learner-centred language teaching aims to bring learners to a point where they reach a degree of autonomy and are able to use the language themselves in real situations outside the classroom. This progression from dependence on the teacher and on the coursebook towards growing confidence and independence is often difficult but it is crucial to the individual success of learners and to the success of teaching programmes. Coursebooks can contribute to achieving this aim by incorporating authentic materials, creating realistic situations and encouraging learners to participate in activities which help develop communicative skills and strategies. By promoting progressively higher levels of autonomy and self-reliance among learners, teaching materials can play an important role in taking them to the threshold of independent language use.

By engaging students' interest and challenging their intellect, coursebooks can provide much of the stimulation which will motivate them to become more independent in their learning and in their use of English. This can be done by including interesting, stimulating topics and by encouraging learners to think for themselves around these topics and discuss them with others.

Guideline Three

Coursebooks should take account of students' needs as learners and should facilitate their learning processes, without dogmatically imposing a rigid 'method'.

Coursebooks help the learner to learn in a number of ways. They select the items to be learned (grammar, functions, skills, etc), break them down into manageable units and sequence them in a way which is designed to lead from the familiar to the unfamiliar and from easier to more difficult items in terms of 'learnability'. Few would disagree that some sort of principled selection and ordering, even if based on intuitive criteria, is necessary.

Coursebooks also embody certain learning styles and strategies, which can influence how individual students go about their own learning. The approach taken by a coursebook towards learning strategies may not be explicit but certain learning styles and strategies will be promoted in the book, explicitly or implicitly, and it is important to identify what they are and how they are put forward.

The approach to learning adopted by a coursebook should not so much impose learning styles as meet students' needs by allowing them to use styles of learning which suit them, where possible encouraging the use of a range of styles so as to offer students some choice in the way they learn. We should be looking increasingly for recognition of individual learning styles by coursebook writers. The teacher's book for *Flying Colours* (Garton-Sprenger and Greenall 1991), for example, notes that 'it is important that learners should develop their own style of learning and take a measure of responsibility for successful language acquisition'. *Flying Colours*, like several other modern coursebooks, contains study advice or learner training aimed at encouraging learners 'to develop positive strategies', thus facilitating the learning process.

Coursebooks can promote learning by contributing to student motivation. Motivation is one of the most powerful forces for good and effective learning and can often be more important than other factors, including teaching method. The teacher's book for *Blueprint One* (Abbs and Freebairn 1990) acknowledges the need for coursebooks to challenge students in order to keep up their motivation:

> For motivation to be sustained, students need to be continually challenged, either linguistically or intellectually, through texts, activities and tasks. Students easily lose concentration if they are allowed to be passive, or if the lessons are too easy or dull. Even at beginners' level, the subject matter must engage the students' minds and challenge them to think.

An interesting coursebook, lively and well presented, with variety of topic and activity can be a powerful factor in strengthening the motivation of the learners, and often of teachers too. Helping students to realize how much progress they have made and encouraging them to review their achievement will also add to motivation and enhance learning. This can be done by periodic quizzes which are designed to show students what they know, rather than what they don't (hence the term *quiz* rather than *test*) and by self-check lists of what students feel that they have learned at various stages through the book.

Guideline Four

Coursebooks should have a clear role as a support for learning. Like teachers, they mediate between the target language and the learner.

Coursebooks facilitate learning, they bring the learner and the target language together, but in a controlled way. Coursebook writers, like learners and teachers, could be said to be participants in the learning/teaching process, albeit at a distance. Coursebooks support the student in a number of ways, but particularly by supplying models of English which are learnable at the student's level of proficiency. They also provide exercises and activities designed to promote fluency in the use of English and they often give explanations or contextualized examples which help learners to understand how the language works.

Coursebooks support teachers by providing ready-made presentation material, ideas for teaching different topics, reading texts, listening passages, dialogues, etc, all carefully graded and accompanied by exercises and activities for class use. They also provide a methodology, or at least an approach to learning.

8   The guidelines in practice: a case study

In order to illustrate in general terms what we might expect to find in a coursebook, and at the same time to examine how the guidelines work in practice, I will look at some characteristics of *Highlight Upper Intermediate* (Vince 1992), the second of a two-part course for intermediate and upper-intermediate adult learners. Coursebooks vary considerably and the features of *Highlight* which will be identified are not the only ones that would be acceptable: they are included here for the purpose of giving practical examples. Other courses can be shown to meet some or all of our expectations in other, equally appropriate ways.

Highlight displays many of the positive features in mainstream courses coming from the major ELT publishers. *Highlight* is aimed at the young adult age range and consists of twelve units, each with a distinct theme, providing material for about 120 hours' work altogether. Our first guideline concerns **aims and objectives.** The stated aims of *Highlight* are:

- **encouraging individual students' input** by inviting opinion and stimulating discussion
- **developing fluency** through functional language practice and balanced skills work
- **improving accuracy** through a practical understanding of grammar
- **consolidating progress** in the 'Study Focus' section which also includes vocabulary and pronunciation work.

A further indication of the aims and objectives of *Highlight* lies in the contents pages, or 'contents map' as it is called in this coursebook. For each unit the contents are displayed under nine headings. The entries for Units 7 and 8 are shown below as examples.

UNIT	TOPIC	LANGUAGE	ACTIVITIES	REA
7	**Many a Slip** Mistakes and Accidents page 55	• Conditional 3: unreal past conditions, negative sentences • *Must have, might have, can't have* • Phrasal verbs • Modal contrasts	• Problem solving • Discussing how an accident could have been avoided • Making deductions about picture situations	• Re jum • *Ac* for s
8	**Town and Around** Towns, houses and traffic page 64	• *Need doing*: describing what is necessary • *Hardly*: meaning *almost not* • Causative *have* • Unreal tenses: wishes for the past • *Instead of* • Conditional sentences	• Planning how to use an old building as a youth centre • Discussing development plans for a town centre • Comparing the plans with the results	• *Lo* for s • *Tra* read

One of the most difficult tasks confronting the coursebook writer is to handle and create material that is at the correct linguistic level, is useful teaching material, forms part of a coherent whole with progression, practises the four skills in a balanced and integrated way **and** is interesting and motivating. This complexity is mirrored by the contents map, which treats a wide range of content categories simultaneously and attempts to show how they fit together and relate to one another.

The main aims of *Highlight* relate to the four language skills taught with particular emphasis on **fluency**, through skills practice, and **accuracy** through an understanding of grammar. Two strands of language-teaching methodology come together here: the **rule-based approach** (understanding of grammar) and the **performance-based approach** (ability to use language effectively with emphasis on the four skills). The accuracy/fluency continuum is also neatly encompassed by linking accuracy to grammatical understanding and fluency to language practice and skills work. The main aims also address student learning needs by giving prominence to the **personalization** of some of the activities in the book, those which ask for students to express their own opinions and give them opportunities to discuss topics suggested to them. Finally, students' learning needs are taken account of by the emphasis on consolidation and recycling in 'Study Focus' sections which provide opportunities for reflection and individual study, thus paving the way for a degree of learner autonomy.

The teacher's book does not set out explicitly the general aims of the course (as opposed to specific teaching objectives for each unit). Students' needs as learners are not discussed in any detail, nor is the role of the teacher. The underlying principles of the course are not stated either, and this is a pity, as a careful reading of these would provide teachers with a useful insight into the

LISTENING	WRITING	SPEAKING	VOCABULARY	PHONOLOGY
● *Dangerous transport and jobs*: listening for specific points ● *A doctor talking*: listening for specific points	● Describing a minor car accident ● Writing about accidents in the home	● Discussing accident prevention ● Role play: describing an accident, discussing causes of accidents	● Word field: *accidents and problems, electricity*	● Words ending in *-er* ● Unstressed syllables
● *Views of London*: listening for main points ● *Traffic problems*: listening for specific points	● Describing a house and neighbourhood ● Writing a letter of complaint about a city area	● Describing facilities in a neighbourhood, describing a town or city ● Role play: discussing development plans for the city traffic problems, the city of the future	● Opposites ● Collocations	● Words ending in *-age* ● '*o*' as /ʌ/

From *Highlight Upper Intermediate*, Vince (Heinemann 1992)

thinking behind the course. Nevertheless the specific teaching objectives set out in the contents and in the teacher's book allow us to build up a picture of a course which has a sound approach and aims to be as comprehensive as possible. This is shown by the attention given not only to grammar (labelled as 'language') but also to vocabulary and phonology. Interestingly, 'functions' do not appear as a category, although several other contemporary courses do make use of this concept. The broader heading of 'activities' is used, and many of the activities included are genuinely communicative.

Moving to our second guideline, concerning the **usefulness** and **relevance** to the learner of the language being taught, we need to look in more detail at the language items included, their balance and organization and whether aspects such as discourse structure and style are taken on board. This is a tall order for the coursebook writer, and we cannot reasonably expect one book to contain everything that we want. What we can expect is a sound general coverage and a reasonable balance. Any special features will be of particular interest and will be worth noting as characteristic of the course.

The language items covered are what would be expected of a course at this level and include general tense work including past, present perfect and past perfect, conditionals, modals, phrasal verbs, relative clauses, etc. Vocabulary gets special attention with some interesting exercises based on word groups, opposites, collocations, etc. There is also attention to pronunciation, with emphasis on areas of particular importance, such as weak forms, word and sentence stress, and some aspects of intonation.

The skills work is particularly comprehensive, with useful activities, based on roleplays and pairwork, for developing oral skills and a lot of well designed guided writing exercises. Reading and listening are also catered for, although, from a presentational point of view, it is a pity that the majority of the reading passages are made to look as though they have been torn from last week's newspaper!

There is some attention given to style and appropriacy, and also occasional work focusing on discourse structure, such as the structuring of written English and the use of conjunctives, referred to as 'text organizers': words such as *although* and *however*. In all, the language content will meet the needs of most learners at this level. Its strength lies in its comprehensive coverage of many aspects of language within one course, together with the range of meaningful learning activities.

The following pages reproduced from *Highlight Upper Intermediate* Student's Book and Teacher's Book show how students are given opportunities to express their own ideas and views (activities 1 and 2) and how spoken English practice is provided through roleplay. The teacher's book gives guidance on setting up and running the pair- and groupwork activities and the roleplay.

Unit 3 Faraway Places

STARTING POINTS

Holiday activities and holiday types

1 What makes a good holiday? Give your opinion of each activity. What are the most popular activities?

HOLIDAY ACTIVITIES

Sunbathing	Walking	Night club
Swimming and diving	Sightseeing	Playing cards
Water sports	Visiting the countryside	Meeting people
Fishing	Museums	Shopping
Team sports	Theatre or cinema	Photography
Skiing	Disco	Relaxing

2 Is it better to have a holiday abroad, or in your own country?

Role play

3 Form a group of four. You want to go on holiday together but have different ideas. Try to come to an agreement.

Student A	Student B
You want to go on a seaside holiday abroad. You are mainly interested in relaxing in the sun because you need a rest after a very busy year.	You want to go on an adventure holiday walking and camping in mountains in your own country. You think this would be a cheap and healthy holiday.

Student C	Student D
You want to relax, but you also want to do some sightseeing. You are interested in museums and old buildings.	Last year you went on a package holiday and spent two weeks on the beach. You want something different this year.

19

From *Highlight Upper Intermediate* Student's Book, Vince (Heinemann 1992)

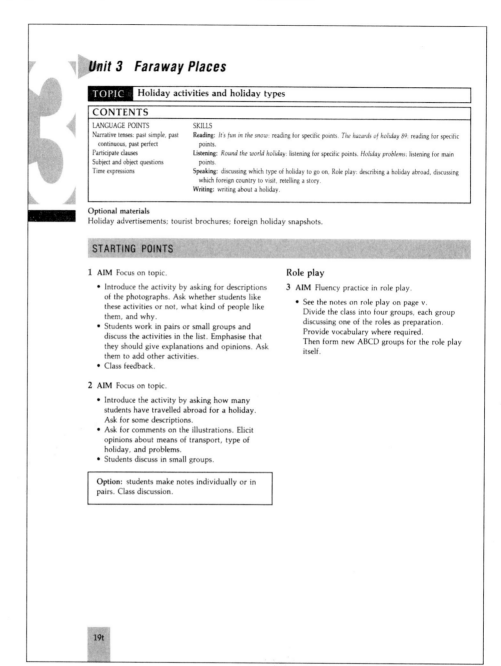

From *Highlight Upper Intermediate* Teacher's Book, Vince (Heinemann 1992)

Our third guideline concerns students' **learning needs** and although very little is said in the introduction to the teacher's book about learners' needs, it is possible to identify a number of features in the book which are relevant here. The material presented is carefully graded with recycling in the student's book and also in the workbook. There are pointers in the student's book to exercises in the workbook which can be done individually outside the classroom or can be used by the teacher as additional material in class.

The selection and grading are basically structural, mainly grammatical in nature, following a conventional sequence of language items. So we find, for example, all three standard conditionals dealt with, as might be expected at this level. The approach to learning is essentially inductive in that the book provides ample contextualized examples of structures and from these examples the learners are expected to hypothesize about the underlying rules. Again, this is the standard approach of most coursebooks. In addition, a grammar reference section is included at the back of the student's book, giving clear and straight-forward explanations of rules, again with plenty of examples. This represents a more deductive approach towards learning, with rules given explicitly. A bridge between the two different approaches is provided by a very useful cross-referencing procedure which points learners towards the reference section at significant points throughout the book. So learners who feel that they need more explanation, or wish to explore a grammar item more thoroughly, are provided with additional resources which they can access quickly and easily through the pointers in the main text. In the example on p 24, the numbers in the boxes refer to the grammar reference section in the student's book.

This allows for some differentiation in how the book is used by different teachers and students by introducing an element of choice, which increases the flexibility of the material. Further choice is offered in the teacher's book through suggestions for alternative activities, ideas on different ways of handling some of the material, and proposed supplementary activities. Motivation is helped by the interesting and varied nature of the topics covered and the way in which these topics form the basis for lively and challenging activities.

We turn now to the final guideline, concerning the **role of the coursebook in promoting effective learning**. We have already seen how *Highlight* provides considerable support to students, whilst allowing them some freedom in how they use the material contained in it. Learning styles are not dogmatically imposed, although a general approach embodying a structural syllabus and a view of learning as primarily an inductive process is implicit.

Support for the teacher is substantial, through a well-designed teacher's book which is interleaved with the student's book, giving a two-page display with the student's book page and the teacher's notes side by side. The purpose of each activity is clearly stated and step-by-step guidance is given on how to use them in class. As mentioned earlier, many suggestions are given for alternative and supplementary activities. Suggested answers are given to most of the exercises and there is a tapescript of all the recorded material.

No coursebook is totally comprehensive and *Highlight* is no exception. Certain aspects of language use, particularly style and discourse structure, are only lightly touched on. We might also like to see a few more substantial reading passages for students at this level, although the author does give advice on using readers and setting up a class library.

LANGUAGE ACTIVITIES

Work situations
Recommending a job

1 Sue is alone in the office, because her colleagues are ill or on holiday and her boss is away. He has left her these notes.

> (a) Don't miss Mr Burns - he'll phone at about 9.45. Copy the sales report and post it to head office. Check how to use the computer and use it to print the receipts
> (b) Take all cheques to the bank. The Post Office closes at 2.00 and the bank at 3.30 today. The photocopier has broken down. Phone for the engineer.
> (c) Send customers receipts for their cheques. Buy some more stamps. Take an hour for lunch any time you like!
> (d) Post all the letters. I will phone you between 11.00 and 11.15. Mr Laing will give you some cash. Take it to the bank.
> (e) Fix a time for today to see Mr Burns. Open all the letters and make a list of cheques received. Check the sales report with Mr. Burns. Change if necessary.

> TO DO
> 9.30 Go to bank
> 11.00 Go to Post Office
> 2.30 Phone about photocopier
> See Mr Burns after lunch (between 3.00 and 4.00)
> Do the receipts, the report and the cash flow book from 4.00 - 5.00.

This is Sue's plan for her day. What is wrong with it?
Unless she sees Mr Burns first she can't go to the bank at 9.30.
She can go to the bank, provided she sees Mr Burns first.
She can't stay at the bank for long, in case Mr Burns phones.

2 After her difficult day, Sue started thinking about other things she could do. What did she say about the good and bad points?

In case ▶ 19
In case is used when we want to be prepared for a situation which might happen.
*I can't go out now **in case** the boss rings.*

Conditional 1 ▶ 7
Provided and **as long as** mean *only if . . .*
Unless means *only if not . . .*
*I'll do it **provided** he agrees.*
*I won't do it **unless** he agrees.*

Conditional 2 ▶ 7
Modals in conditional sentences
*If I **studied** I **could become** a teacher.*
*If I **were** a teacher, I **might** not like it.*

29

From *Highlight Upper Intermediate*, Vince (Heinemann 1992)

Chapter 3 The coursebook package

This chapter will look at what coursebooks contain and the make-up of the total package, as coursebooks seldom stand alone.

1 The make-up of the coursebook package

Our concern here is the whole learning package: how it is made up and how the different parts relate to one another. I have used the term 'coursebook' to refer to any integrated package of materials with the coursebook at the centre, but we also need to consider how the central coursebook is supported by the other materials.

Most course packages consist of at least a student's book and a teacher's book. The student's book is probably thought of as the main plank of a package, and rightly so as it is the main point of contact with the student. However, teachers' books are also very important and are responsible for providing teachers with the detailed information that they need in order to make the best use of the whole course.

Workbooks or activity books are also commonly included in course packages and are intended to give students extra practice in items already introduced in class. They often give additional writing practice and are produced fairly cheaply so that they can be written in and thrown away when completed.

Cassettes normally figure prominently in course packages, and are generally used for listening and pronunciation work. It is important to listen to the cassettes when evaluating this aspect of the package, as the quality of the material recorded on them can vary a lot.

A major consideration is the extent to which the different parts of the course package truly work together to form an integrated package (a term used very frequently by those responsible for promotional copywriting in ELT publishing). Ideas on how to bring the different parts together and suggestions on how and when the various components are best used should appear in the teacher's book. Ideally we would look for a chart or other schematic representation showing the progression of each component in relation to the other components.

Clearly some parts of a package are more central than others, and material that in some packages is contained in the student's book will be found in other packages in a separate book. Tests are a good example of this.

Most budgets for purchasing teaching materials are limited, so it is important to know which parts of a package are essential, and which are optional. The students' and teachers' books would be difficult to dispense with, and it would be a pity not to have access to a set of authentic-sounding cassettes for listening work and pronunciation practice. On the other hand, some parts of the package can very definitely be seen as optional extras, without which the course can still be used effectively. Video material, when it accompanies general courses, normally comes into this category. It is rarely central to the teaching of the main language points, but serves rather for recycling language in different contexts and for maintaining interest and motivation in the learners. This is valuable but not essential, and sometimes the distinction has to be made, so that priorities can be decided for materials purchase.

The following extracts give examples of the make-up of some typical courses.

Course components and organisation

Flying Colours is a classroom-based course which will take adult and young adult beginners to intermediate level in three stages. The course components at each stage are:

Students' Book
Workbook
Teacher's Book
Class cassettes
Language Study cassettes

From *Flying Colours* Teacher's Book 2, Garton-Sprenger and Greenall (Heinemann 1991)

The New Cambridge English Course is designed for people who are learning English for general practical or cultural purposes. The course generally presupposes a European-type educational background, but with some adaptation it can be used successfully with learners from other cultural environments. The course teaches British English, but illustrates other varieties as well.

The material at each level includes a Student's Book, a Teacher's Book and a set of Class Cassettes (for classwork); a Practice Book, with or without Key (for homework); two optional Student's Cassettes; and an optional Test Book for teachers. Split editions of the Student's Book, Practice Book and Student's Cassettes are also available.

A set of two video cassettes and an accompanying Teacher's Guide are also available for use with Level 1. The Teacher's Guide contains photocopiable tasks for students to use with the video. For teachers who do not wish to photocopy, a Teacher's Guide without tasks and separate Student's Activity Books are available.

From *The New Cambridge English Course* Teacher's Book 1, Swan and Walter (CUP 1990)

At each level *Grapevine* comprises:

Student's Book with an introductory unit, forty double-page units, four Stories for pleasure, grammar summaries, a vocabulary index, list of irregular verbs, and a listening appendix.

Workbooks A and B providing further reading and writing activities.

Interleaved Teacher's Book with detailed and flexible lesson plans.

Stereo Cassettes including dialogues, texts, songs, and listening development.

Video integrated into the course as a stimulating option for both presentation and review.

Video Activity Book including full exploitation material, language summaries, transcripts, a guide to using video in the classroom, and teaching notes.

From *Grapevine* Teacher's Book 1, Viney and Viney (OUP 1990)

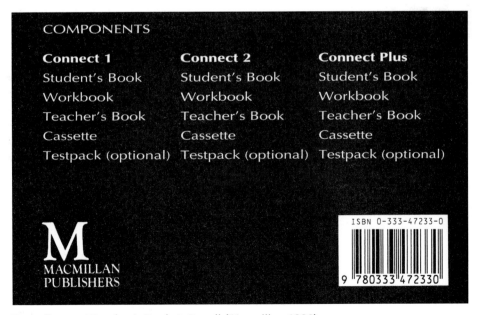

From *Connect* Teacher's Book 1, Revell (Macmillan 1990)

Checklist for the make-up of courses

☐ What are the components which make up the total course package?
  - student's book
  - teacher's book
  - workbook or activity book
  - tests
  - additional reading material
  - additional listening material
  - cassettes for listening
  - cassettes for pronunciation
  - video
  - CALL materials
  - other components

☐ How well do the different parts relate to the whole? Is there an overall guide to using the package? Is there cross-referencing between the different parts?

☐ Which parts are essential and which are optional?

2   The organization of coursebooks

Our next concern is with the amount of continuity within the materials and the routes through the materials which are available to learners.

It is rarely sufficient for students to meet new items only once. In the case of grammar and vocabulary, items not only need to be met in context and actively practised, they need to be recycled three, four or more times before they become stored in the long-term memory. One principle of recycling is that items are encountered in a structured way on several occasions in different contexts. In this way students learn the form and the sound of a language item (grammatical form or lexical item) through progressive exposure, and by meeting it in a number of different contexts they develop an increasing understanding of its use and meaning.

We would expect a general course to have a clear policy on recycling, with progressive reinforcement of newly taught items. It is useful to have a record, for instance, of where a vocabulary item is first introduced and then when it is used on subsequent occasions. As a basic principle of learning is to move from the familiar to the new, and to relate new items to those already known, recycling of previously taught items can be linked to the first presentation of a new item. For example, the present continuous form of the verb, already presented and practised in context, can be recycled at the same time as it is contrasted with the present simple.

Many teachers and students are happier when they have a straightforward route through a course, and they sometimes feel more secure when the conventional beginning-to-end direction is used. There are, however, alternatives which, when carefully used, give more flexibility. An example of this is *The Sourcebook* (Shepherd and Cox 1991) which is designed to give users greater flexibility in designing their own syllabus. To this end *The Sourcebook* offers students three separate sections: grammar, vocabulary and skills. The skills section gives practice in language use, and has cross-referencing to the other two sections for language study.

INTRODUCTION

These notes about *The Sourcebook* are for students and teachers.

A philosophical guide

Students and teachers all work in different ways – this book encourages learning and teaching English in your own way.

Many course books dictate to the learner and the teacher what should be learned, in what order and in what way. *The Sourcebook* is different. It has been designed to be flexible, to suit the teacher and the course being taught, and to give the student a book he or she can use for self-study as well as in class.

A practical guide

HOW THIS BOOK IS MADE UP:

STARTING OUT
Introducing each other, the language we need and how to learn it

GRAMMAR
Functions, nouns, verbs, prepositions and sentences

VOCABULARY
Key words, word groups and exercises

SKILLS
Listening, speaking, reading and writing presented in 10 topic areas

HOW TO USE THE BOOK

IN CLASS A typical course begins with **Starting out**. After that, the items in **Grammar** and **Vocabulary** can be used *when* and *how* it suits the course, but the **Skills** part (10 units) is designed to be used in class and can be used in the order given in the book. The units in **Skills** are cross-referenced to relevant pages in **Vocabulary** and **Grammar**.

FOR SELF-STUDY AND REVISION The student can also use the **Grammar** and **Vocabulary** parts for his or her own reference. There is a key to both parts at the back of the book.

TEACHERS AND COURSE DESIGNERS will find these materials are adaptable to many different teaching situations and syllabuses. It is important that teachers familiarise themselves with the contents and design of the book. The Teacher's Book contains many ideas on different ways of using *The Sourcebook*.

6

From *The Sourcebook Pre-intermediate*, Shepherd and Cox (Longman 1991)

There is no linear route through this book. The teacher, the class or the individual student must find their own way through by selecting appropriate material from the sections and putting together a negotiated syllabus which in all probability will grow organically as the learners progress. The book is not graded in a structural way as in more conventional courses, but offers its contents for selection on a 'self-service' basis. To help users, there is an extensive and detailed learner-training section which gives detailed advice and guidance to students on how to use the book.

Clearly this alternative is not for students lacking confidence or teachers lacking experience. However, it is an interesting initiative which would be of value to students on a 'false beginners' or revision course and to teachers with classes of students having widely varying needs. A degree of sophistication is needed to handle material of this kind, and a good deal more responsibility falls on students when they contribute to the design of their own syllabuses.

Checklist for the organization of coursebooks

- ☐ How is continuity maintained in the materials?
- ☐ What techniques are used for recycling and reinforcement of learning?
- ☐ How is earlier learning developed or refined in later sections of the material?
- ☐ What route is the learner expected to take through the material? Is there one predetermined route, or are alternatives/optional routes given?
- ☐ Are there reference sections? If so, are there pointers to them in the main text? Are they well integrated?
- ☐ Is there an index of language items?
- ☐ Is there a list of new vocabulary? If so, does it show where each word is first introduced?
- ☐ Is the material suitable for use in a self-study mode? Does it have a key to exercises?
- ☐ If it is a new course, are all components published and available? If it is not yet complete, will the next levels be ready when you need them?

Chapter 4 The language content

In this chapter we are concerned with the language that is contained in the coursebook, with **what** is being taught (as opposed to **how** it is taught, which will be considered in Chapter 8). This language content can then be compared with what the students **need** to learn and **expect** to learn, in order to evaluate the suitability of the material so far as its language content is concerned.

1 Language form and language use

Coursebooks are concerned with the teaching and learning of the language itself, in some or all of its aspects. Themes, topics, communicative strategies, cultural issues and other factors are also important and will be discussed later in this book. But the actual items of language taught – grammar, vocabulary and phonology – form the foundation of everything else that contributes to the complex process of language teaching.

It is generally necessary to analyse language and divide it into small units for effective teaching and learning to take place. Yet it is notoriously difficult to separate individual aspects of language from the whole, and isolate them, without losing authenticity and naturalness in the process. This is mainly because language is a complex phenomenon which operates at several levels simultaneously. For example, speakers have to express what they mean through the grammatical, lexical and phonological systems of the language simultaneously and also have to select appropriate communicative strategies. They also have to interpret what is being said to them, using the same processes in reverse. The 'whole' of language in use is greater than the sum of its parts.

This goes some way towards explaining one of the most difficult problems in language teaching and particularly in designing materials. Students cannot be expected to handle several different aspects of a new foreign language simultaneously, when they are just beginning to learn it. To some degree the acquired skills of language use will be transferable from the mother tongue, but even so it is essential to reduce the learning load in the foreign language to assimilable units, and this invariably entails focusing on different aspects of the language separately. So, part of a lesson may concentrate on teaching a new grammatical form and another part may focus on vocabulary development. The lesson may finish with some skills work – practising listening, for example. Coursebooks mirror this approach by focusing selectively on different aspects of language form and language use. Language is analysed and broken down into small units for teaching purposes. An essential question for teachers and materials writers is how far a language can be analysed and fragmented in this way without losing its nature and identity.

2   Grammar

The first considerations are what grammar items are included and how far they correspond to learner needs. Grammar is a major component of any general language course, whether it is acknowledged as such, or disguised as something else. It is the effective teaching of grammar that distinguishes a true language course from a phrasebook and it is an understanding of and an ability to use grammar that equips learners with the ability to create their own utterances and use language for their own purposes.

When introducing new grammar items, it is possible to teach the form of a new grammatical item without its meaning (in the sense of its underlying use), as in the following example of teaching the article taken from *Blueprint One* (Abbs and Freebairn 1990), where the focus is on the **form** of the indefinite article (*a/an*).

GRAMMAR FOCUS

Indefinite article		**Definite article**	**Plurals**
a desk	**an** apple	**the** pen	(the) pens
a pen	**an** orange	**the** apple	(the) apples

When do you use *an*?
What letter makes a word plural?

From *Blueprint One*, Abbs and Freebairn (Longman 1990)

Equally, it is possible to present a new grammar item with emphasis on its use, minimizing or postponing the problems presented by its form (or forms in the case of irregular verbs). In the example of the past simple tense on p 33 taken from *Signature Elementary* (Phillips and Sheerin 1990), a number of regular and irregular past simple tense forms are introduced through the reading passage before the form of the tense is explained to the students, focusing attention at this stage primarily on the **use** of the tense.

Both books redress the balance subsequently and cover the missing aspect (form or use), but it is interesting to note that the sequences are different. There is clearly no correct sequence, and sequencing will vary according to learner level, the nature of the item to be learned and the preferences of the coursebook writers. It is however indisputable that both form and use must be learned, and as closely together as possible.

Working days

1 Reading

Mary Lacy was a maid in a big house in London from 1912 until 1915. Here is her story. Read the text and find the answers to these questions:

1 Was Mary happy at the big house?
2 What new job did Mary want?

I was born in 1900. When I was twelve, I started work as a maid in a big house. Every morning, at five o'clock, I washed in icy cold water and got dressed. Then I went downstairs and cooked breakfast. After breakfast, I washed the dishes and cleaned all the rooms.

At half past seven every morning I helped the young lady of the house to get dressed. I carried up hot water for her to wash with. I laid out her clothes and combed her hair. She was twelve years old like me, but she pulled my hair and called me names. One day she stabbed me in the hand with a needle. I asked her to be kind to me, but nothing changed. Why did she hate me?

I worked very hard every day until nine or ten o'clock at night and I only had one day off a month. I did all the cleaning in the house and they paid me very little. I hated it.

One day, in 1915, I learned that they wanted women workers in the factories because of the war. The hours were short (from eight o'clock in the morning to seven o'clock at night) and the pay was very good. So I decided to run away.

That night, I waited until everybody was asleep. At one o'clock I opened my door carefully and listened. I walked downstairs quietly with my shoes in my hand, reached the front door and pushed it open. Then I closed it quietly behind me. Free at last!

A Read through the text again and write down:

1 five jobs Mary did every day at the big house
2 three things Mary didn't like about her work
3 all the verbs in the first paragraph. What do you notice?

B Work with a partner and talk about the answers to these questions:

1 Why did Mary wash in icy cold water?
2 Why did Mary decide to leave?
3 Why did she wait until everyone was asleep?
4 Why did Mary think the working hours in the factory were short?

2 Language Practice

A Look at Language Study 1.5.
Notice how to make questions in the past with *Did . . . + verb*. Now make up five questions about Mary's life, write them down and then ask a partner your questions. Answer: 'Yes, she did' or 'No, she didn't.'

B Read the story and put the verbs into the past tense:

On Monday morning my day 1 *started* in the usual way. At seven o'clock I 2 . . . . . . (*get up*), 3 . . . . (*wash*), and 4 . . . . . . (*comb*) my hair. Then I 5 . . . . . . (*go downstairs*) and 6 . . . . . . (*have*) breakfast. At half past seven I 7 . . . . . . (*walk*) to the bus stop and 8 . . . . . . (*wait*) for the bus. I 9 . . . . . . (*wait*) for half an hour, but the bus didn't come. Then one of my friends 10 . . . . . . (*walk*) by. 'Why are you waiting at the bus stop? You know there aren't any buses on Sunday!'

3 Pronunciation and Spelling

A Say whether the past tense of the following verbs has one syllable or two:

hurry	call	start	walk	close
stop	hate	help	want	stay

B Look at Language Study 5.3. Write eight sentences with the past tense of these verbs.

25

From *Signature Elementary*, Phillips and Sheerin (Nelson 1990)

Checklist for grammar items

- ☐ What grammar items are included? Do they correspond to students' language needs?
- ☐ Are they presented in small enough units for easy learning?
- ☐ Is there an emphasis on language form?
- ☐ Is there an emphasis on language use (meaning)?
- ☐ How balanced is the treatment of form and use?
- ☐ Are newly introduced items related to and contrasted with items already familiar to the learners?
- ☐ Where one grammatical form has more than one meaning (eg the present continuous), are all relevant meanings taught (not necessarily together)?

3 Evaluating the grammar content: a case study

A useful way of gaining insight into coursebooks and, where necessary, comparing them, is to identify some grammatical points that are difficult to teach and pose problems for your learners. Which points are selected will depend on your own students and your teaching situation. Two grammar items that are generally problematic are the present perfect verb form and the definite and indefinite articles. In both cases, the actual form of language involved is not such a problem, but the use of the items is difficult because abstract concepts are involved. In the case of the present perfect, the underlying meaning can be summed up as 'past with present relevance or effect'. As far as articles are concerned, the choice of definite or indefinite article (or in certain cases no article) depends largely on whether the entity being referred to is already known and identifiable to the listener (definite article) or not (indefinite article).

We would expect to find these items dealt with thoroughly and clearly at the appropriate level, with comprehensible contextualization which will lead learners to understand and internalize the underlying meaning. We have briefly looked at one treatment of the article (above). Let us now take a look at how the present perfect is handled in two different courses.

In *Blueprint One* (Abbs and Freebairn 1990) the present perfect is presented for the first time in Unit 32, which is reproduced on p 35.

As can be seen, the new verb form is presented in context, using visuals in the coursebook and a listening passage on cassette. There is also a box, showing how the present perfect is constructed in its affirmative, negative and interrogative forms. Irregular past participle endings are given in Exercise 2. The forms of the present perfect are practised in Exercises 2 and 4 and something of the underlying meaning comes over from the contexts of presentation and practice. Further practice is given in the workbook and an overview of form and meaning is given in the *Language review*, reproduced on p 36.

32
Recent events

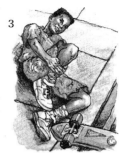

2 Use the list of verbs to say what has happened in each picture.

break	broke	broken
lose	lost	lost
drop	dropped	dropped
hurt	hurt	hurt
find	found	found
see	saw	seen

A: What has he done?
B: He's broken a cup.

1 cup   3 leg
2 magazine   4 £5

1 🔲 LISTENING

Before you listen

Mrs Gibson has just had some good news.
What do you think has happened?

1 She has just won a competition.
2 She has just passed an exam.
3 She has just received some money.

Now listen and find out why Mrs Gibson is so happy.

3 🔲 SPEECHWORK

Listen and repeat these words. Notice the /h/ sound.

he's   his   have   has   had
here   hair   hurt
he's had a nice time   he's hurt his leg

4 Mime something unfortunate which has just happened to you, e.g. you've just broken your watch. Other students guess what it is by asking *Yes/No* questions.

A: Have you lost something?
B: No, I haven't.
A: Have you broken something?
B: Yes, I have.

GRAMMAR FOCUS: **Present perfect tense**	
Question What has she/he won?	*Positive* She/He has (just) won a competition.
	Negative She/He hasn't won a competition.
Has she/he won?	*Short answer* Yes, she/he has. No, she/he hasn't.

111

From *Blueprint One*, Abbs and Freebairn (Longman 1990)

Language review

PRESENT PERFECT SIMPLE

Positive statements			*Negative statements*		
I've	finished.		I	haven't	finished.
We've			We		
They've			They		
She's			She	hasn't	
He's			He		

Question			*Short answer* *Positive*			*Short answer* *Negative*		
Have	you	finished?	Yes,	I	have.	No,	I	haven't.
	we			we			we	
	they			they			they	
Has	she			she	has.		she	hasn't.
	he			he			he	

1 In this book the present perfect simple is used to express:
   recent events   *He's broken a cup.*   (Unit 32)
   experiences   *Have you ever been to Africa?*   (Unit 33)
                    He's been to Rio twice.
2 This tense cannot be used to talk about events which happened at a
   specific time in the past, e.g. You cannot say: ~~I have finished it yesterday~~.

From *Blueprint One*, Abbs and Freebairn (Longman 1990)

The presentation in the student's book is clear and is based on an inductive
approach (ie from examples, the learners work out the rule). Explanations are
only given in the *Language review*, and then only briefly. The emphasis is on
the language form and on one of its uses: to refer to recent events. The more
difficult aspect of the meaning of the present perfect, the underlying concept
of 'past with present relevance', is not taught at this stage. This is an
elementary level coursebook and the writers deal with other uses of the present
perfect at pre-intermediate and intermediate levels.

The Sourcebook Pre-intermediate (Shepherd and Cox 1991) uses contextualized
examples, but to a lesser extent, and has a more developed explanation of the
form, and particularly the underlying meaning of the present perfect, as can
be seen from the page reproduced on p 37.

The approach here, although inductive to a certain degree, is more deductive
(ie giving explanations and rules, rather than encouraging learners to work the
rules out for themselves) than in *Blueprint One*. It provides a similar amount of
practice material, which is contextualized in the coursebook through the use of
visuals, etc.

Such an approach is likely to suit rather more advanced students or 'false
beginners', certainly those who have enough English to understand the
explanations and rules, however clearly and simply these are presented.

VERBS

Tenses 3

Present perfect:

since

for

ever

never

been

gone

LOOK

Julia **has** finish**ed** typing the report.
Has she finished the letters?
No, she **has**n't start**ed** them.

CHECK

1 Complete these sentences with forms of these verbs:

finish   cook   wash   clean

It's nearly time for lunch. How is the housework getting on?

It's nearly finished. Peter _____ up all the plates, Mary and Jane _____ the windows, and Norman _____ the lunch. Jimmy is still sweeping the floor, he _____ that job yet.

GRAMMAR

The past tense refers to past time . . .	. . . and the present tense refers to present time . . .
They cleaned the windows **half an hour ago**.	The windows are clean **now**.

The present perfect joins past time and present time . . .

They **have** clean**ed** the windows.

We use the present perfect tense when we are interested *now* in the *result* of an action which happened (or at least began) in the past.

With a reference to past time like 'yesterday' or 'at 5 o'clock' we cannot use the present perfect. 'I have seen him at 5 o'clock' is not possible. This would be 'I **saw him** at 5 o'clock'.

PRACTICE

2 Look at this chart, then complete the sentences:

FOUR FRIENDS PREPARE FOR A TRIP TO THE BEACH

Winston:	check the oil	✓	Jane:	buy fruit	✓
	fill up with petrol	X		pack the picnic basket	X
Elizabeth:	make lemonade	✓	Mark:	make the sandwiches	X
	find the map	X		pump up the ball	✓

E: Jane, *have* you *bought* the fruit yet?
J: Yes, I have, but I _____ the picnic basket.
E: Why not?
J: Well, Mark _____ the sandwiches yet. But he _____ the ball!
E: We don't need a ball! This is a beach trip, not a football match! I _____ the lemonade – it's ready, but I _____ the map. Has anyone seen it?
W: The map is in the car.
E: Is the car ready? _____ you _____ it up with petrol?
W: No, we can do that on the way, but I _____ the oil – we are almost ready to leave!

From *The Sourcebook Pre-intermediate*, Shepherd and Cox (Longman 1991)

4   Vocabulary

Until recent years, vocabulary was a neglected area of foreign language teaching, but it has gained its due recognition in the last few years, as realization came that sustained communication is virtually impossible without access to a relevant and fairly wide range of vocabulary. It is often asserted with some truth that, particularly at lower levels, students can communicate more effectively with a knowledge of vocabulary than with a knowledge of grammar.

Selecting vocabulary is a tricky subject and not as simple as might be expected. One criterion alone (such as frequency) is inadequate for selecting a workable vocabulary range for a teaching programme or coursebook. Few coursebooks explain how the vocabulary they include has been selected, beyond general statements referring to frequency and usefulness. An illuminating account of how a relatively complex selection system was built up can be found in the *Cambridge English Lexicon* (Hindmarsh 1980).

In general terms, we would expect to see at least 1000 new words taught in each stage of a general course, where a stage represents 120–140 hours' work. Very often additional vocabulary-learning activities are provided in the students' workbook, as much vocabulary learning can take place outside the classroom. Because the vocabulary of English is so large, we can only expect a fraction of it to be included in any coursebook.

As well as teaching as many new words as possible, coursebooks can help equip students with strategies for handling the unfamiliar vocabulary that they will inevitably meet. They can also enable students to develop their own vocabulary-learning strategies. This is a powerful approach and can be based on sensitization to the systems of vocabulary, encouragement of sound dictionary skills and reflection on effective learning techniques.

Nearly all modern courses include vocabulary-learning activities in their provision, though with varying degrees of prominence. It is worth examining the nature of the activities and exercises to ensure that they help learners to extend and develop their vocabulary in a purposeful and structured way. We would not expect to see just wordlists or dictionary definitions of new words. Nor would we expect to see words taught in isolation or outside of context. Rather we would look for exercises which sensitize learners to the structure of the lexicon of English and to the various relationships that exist within it.

Good vocabulary development activities tend to exploit some or all of the following:

- semantic relations – word groups according to meaning, synonyms, hyponyms, opposites
- situational relationships – word sets associated with particular situations, eg sport, transport, politics
- collocations – words commonly found in association, eg *food and drink, for better or worse,* also noun + preposition links and phrasal verbs (verb + particle links)
- relationships of form (often referred to as 'word building'), eg *long, length, lengthen.*

Some courses distinguish usefully between active and passive vocabulary.

The following are examples of vocabulary-teaching material at advanced and elementary levels.

UNIT 1

E **Vocabulary**

Neutral and strong adjectives

1 Study the following language items from D Reading 2, and discuss the questions below them. Check your answers on Study page 158.

Adverbs	Adjectives
quite	reputable
very	useful
downright	atrocious

a Which adverb is strongest and which weakest?
b Which adjective is strongest?
c Which of the following adverbs could replace which of the adverbs in the first column with little change of meaning?
absolutely   fairly   extremely   utterly
d Fill in the table, using the adjectives beneath it.

surprising	amazing
	atrocious
	indispensable
angry	
	ridiculous
hungry	starving

silly   useful   bad   furious

e What is the difference between the adjectives on the left and those on the right?
f Which adjectives follow adverbs like *downright*? Which follow *very*, etc.?

From *Nexus*, Mills (Heinemann 1990)

FOCUS ON WORDS

5.1

❶

THE BIG DAY OUT
FOR ALL THE FAMILY

SPEND THE DAY AT WEMBLEY

THE BEST CIRCUS IN TOWN

HARRY BLACK'S

CIRCUS

Come and see our main attractions

SARAH BLACK and her beautiful LIBERTY HORSES

DANA and her famous crocodiles

PUSHKA on the high trapeze

ROLY AND HIS FRIENDLY CLOWNS

LEO and his ferocious LIONS

JACK & JILL OUR FANTASTIC ACROBATS

Come and Talk to the Animals at COLCHESTER ZOO

SPEND A DAY WITH US

DON'T MISS OUR DAILY PRESENTATIONS

SNAKE HANDLING	1100	1400	1815	in the PARROT TENT
PENGUIN PARADE	1200	1630		from the PENGUIN POOL
CHIMPANZEE'S TEA PARTY	1230	1600		in the MAIN TENT
ELEPHANT TRICKS	1245	1530		in the ELEPHANT HOUSE
PARROT DISPLAY	1245	1445	1545	at the PARROT TENT
FEEDING THE SEALS	1300	1600		at the SEAL POOL

❷

FINDING NEW WORDS

1   Give your opinion
■ Texts **1** and **2** come from leaflets advertising things you can do at weekends. Read them. Which do you prefer? Why?

2   Find new words
▶ Read Text **1**. Find
• words for circus attractions
• names of animals
Read Text **2**. Make two lists of
• names of animals you know
• names of animals you don't know
▶◀ Compare lists. Help each other with the words you don't know.

3   Check
■ Check with your teacher as in the example.

Does X mean Y?

you

36

From *Freewheeling 2*, Rodriguez and Barbisan (Heinemann 1992)

▨ Checklist for vocabulary

- ☐ Is vocabulary-learning material included in its own right? If so, how prominent is it? Is it central to the course or peripheral?
- ☐ How much vocabulary is taught?
- ☐ Is there any principled basis for selection of vocabulary?
- ☐ Is there any distinction between active and passive vocabulary, or classroom vocabulary?
- ☐ Is vocabulary presented in a structured, purposeful way?
- ☐ Are learners sensitized to the structure of the lexicon through vocabulary-learning exercises based on:
  - – semantic relationships
  - – formal relationships
  - – collocations
  - – situation-based word groups?
- ☐ Does the material enable students to expand their own vocabularies independently by helping them to develop their own learning strategies?

5 **Phonology**

The teaching of pronunciation is another item, like vocabulary, that tended in the past to be sidelined in many general courses. However, most recent courses include the teaching of phonology to a greater or lesser extent. Most of them cover the articulation of individual sounds, word stress, sentence stress and some aspects of intonation. Weak forms and connected speech are often given prominence.

Emphasis should be at least as much on the global aspects of phonology – weak forms, stress, rhythm – as on producing individual sounds, because the production of natural-sounding connected speech depends on the speaker's ability to handle the sentence stress and intonation of English with some degree of appropriateness. These systems will most probably operate in English quite differently from the way they are used in the learners' mother tongues. English, as a stress-timed language, operates at the level of sentence stress very differently from syllable-timed languages, and intonation patterns are not usually transferable across languages with their original meanings and expression of attitudes intact.

In the case of both individual sounds and connected speech, there should not be excessive emphasis on absolute correctness, or virtual native-speaker accuracy. Rather, there should be an awareness of areas where misunderstandings can most easily occur and a focus on avoiding such unfortunate occurrences. For instance, in German a fall–rise intonation can express enthusiasm and keenness, whereas in English it can convey uncertainty or lack of interest. Mapping the German fall–rise onto a response to an invitation in English, such as 'Yes, OK then' can convey the opposite of what is intended, signalling reluctance or indifference rather than the intended warmth and enthusiasm.

The use of specialized terminology (such as *voiced/unvoiced sounds, weak forms, stressed syllables*) is essential if learners are going to study phonology in any depth, but may be unnecessary if the treatment is relatively incidental. It must be left to individual teachers to decide if the time spent on learning such technical terms is justified. The same must apply to learning grammatical terminology.

As a general principle though, learners should be given terminology whenever it will help them to analyse English, categorize it and as a consequence understand better how it works. This principle applies equally to the use of the phonemic alphabet and we should see whether the coursebook uses it and includes it for reference.

Diagrams showing stress and intonation are used in some courses and not in others, although most writers do not insist dogmatically that their view is imposed against the teacher's judgement. *Headway Intermediate Pronunciation* uses a simple but effective way of showing sentence stress and intonation (which are really inseparable features) as shown below:

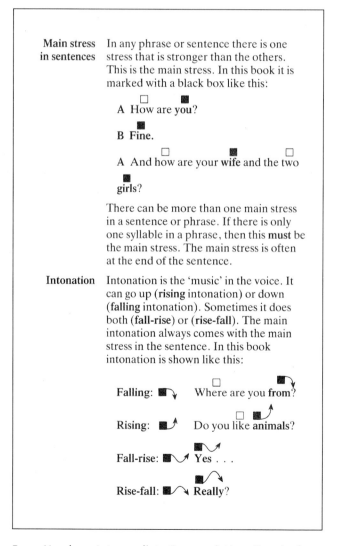

From *Headway Intermediate Pronunciation*, Cunningham and Bowler (OUP 1990)

Grapevine (Viney, P. and K. 1990) avoids

> the use of stress and intonation diagrams, as they can often cause confusion for students and teachers alike, though occasionally simple arrows can be employed to denote rising or falling intonation. A cassette recording is the best way of noting stress, rhythm and intonation. If you are happy with diagrams and gestures to demonstrate patterns, use them. If not, concentrate on the recordings.

A final but very important question concerns the cassettes that accompany pronunciation-teaching material. It is essential that the language recorded on them provides a good model for learners, that weak forms are used where they are supposed to be, that sentence stress is natural and that intonation is appropriately used.

Checklist for phonology

- ☐ How thoroughly and systematically are each of the following aspects of the phonological system covered:
    - – articulation of individual sounds
    - – words in contact (eg assimilation)
    - – word stress
    - – weak forms
    - – sentence stress
    - – intonation?
- ☐ Where phonology is taught selectively, is the emphasis on areas of pronunciation that are important to meet learners' needs and help avoid misunderstandings?
- ☐ Is the pronunciation work built on to other types of work, such as listening, dialogue practice, etc or does it stand separately?
- ☐ How much terminology is used? Is it comprehensible to the learners?
- ☐ Is the phonemic alphabet used? If so, are students given any training in learning it?
- ☐ Does the material use a diagrammatic system to show stress and intonation?
- ☐ Are there cassettes for pronunciation practice? If so, do they provide good models for learners?

6 Integration of pronunciation teaching with other work

Courses differ in the extent to which they integrate pronunciation work with other work. *Upper Intermediate Matters* (Bell and Gower 1992) adopts an integrative approach, as is explained in the teacher's book:

> Pronunciation
> Many of the exercises come out of the text in the first cycle of the unit or out of vocabulary work. Usually, it is suggested that on-going attention is given to pronunciation rather than devoting specific lessons to this area of language.

Significant areas of phonology are covered in this way, by a combination of specialized pronunciation exercises and focus on aspects of pronunciation in other exercises and activities.

An alternative approach is adopted by *Headway Intermediate* (Soars, J. and L. 1986) where relatively little attention is given to pronunciation in the main course, but significant problem areas are signalled in the teacher's book to forewarn teachers that they need to concentrate on pronunciation while, for example, presenting grammar items. An example of this comes with the introduction of the past simple:

There are three pronunciations of **-ed** at the end of regular past simple verbs.
/t/ after unvoiced sounds   *washed hoped worked*
/d/ after voiced sounds   *married opened lived*
/ɪd/ after /t/ and /d/   *wanted started ended.*

There are no exercises in the student's book to focus attention on this difficult feature, or to practise it. However, a separate part of the course package, *Headway Intermediate Pronunciation* (Cunningham and Bowler 1990), came out four years later and now provides very comprehensive material for teaching all aspects of pronunciation. Although linked to the sequencing and structure of *Headway Intermediate*, it claims that it can be used easily with other courses both for class use and for individual study. The beginning of Unit 3, reproduced below, shows how the pronunciation point that was originally simply referred to in the teacher's book forms the basis of a specific recognition exercise.

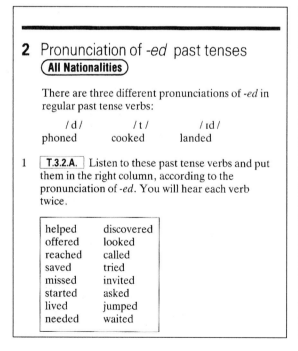

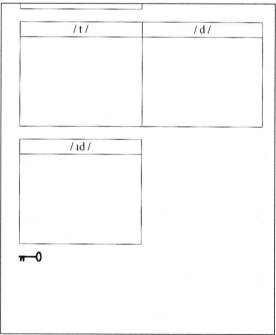

From *Headway Intermediate Pronunciation*, Cunningham and Bowler (OUP 1990)

The spelling of English must present a bewildering problem to many foreign learners, yet scant attention is paid to it in perhaps the majority of courses. Students tend to be left to sort it out for themselves, simply learning the spellings of words on a one-off basis, or by analogy to words with similar sounds. Analogy, unfortunately, is a poor guide in many cases, as the trio *bear, bean* and *steak* will testify. Sound–spelling relationships in English are a minefield, and as yet incompletely described by linguistics. So it is no surprise that many coursebook writers steer clear of the whole area. However, even though we may be in no position to provide a comprehensive and painless guide to English spelling, some guidance through the maze by identifying common sound–spelling relationships can be of great help to students in their writing and reading. Too much would be tedious and demotivating, because the basics of spelling operate at micro level below the level of meaning, but the occasional focus on sound–spelling relationships can pay dividends, as in the following example from *Third Dimension* (O'Neill and Mugglestone 1989).

---

6 Words and sounds

Pronounce these groups of words aloud. Pay particular attention to the letters in **bold**. In which word is the sound of these letters different?

1 p**ea**s cr**ea**m br**ea**d b**ea**n
2 br**ea**d p**e**pper l**e**ntil l**ea**n
3 b**ea**n b**ee**f ch**ee**se p**ea**r
4 b**ee**f m**ea**l p**i**zza b**ee**r
5 f**i**sh ch**i**p r**i**pe f**i**llet
6 c**a**ke st**ea**k v**ea**l b**a**ke

- How many of the words above can you find that have the same sound as *ea* in these three words: p**ea**, st**ea**k, br**ea**d?
- Think of at least three more words (they don't have to be about food) that have the same *ea* sound as in p**ea**r.

From *Third Dimension*, O'Neill and Mugglestone (Longman 1989)

7 Discourse

I am using the term discourse here in a general way to refer to the features of language use that go beyond the domain of grammar rules and include areas such as the sequencing of sentences, cohesion, paragraphing, structuring text, participation in conversations, etc. Studies in text cohesion, discourse analysis and conversational analysis provide much of the theoretical and analytical basis for understanding this area, which focuses on *language use* and the conventions that structure how we use language for effective communication. So it is directly relevant to the communicative approach.

Virtually all coursebooks will present models of discourse, consciously or not, through the examples of language that they offer in dialogues, reading texts and listening passages. Particularly at elementary level and lower-intermediate level, the language will be limited in its range and complexity. Consequently, the discourse structure will also be restricted in range and complexity. However, we should look for models that represent authentic discourse, even though at a simplified level.

A reading text, for example, should display some of the features of authentic text, such as coherent structuring of content, paragraphing and appropriate use of cohesive devices, including pronouns for anaphoric reference and conjunctives. The range of conjunctives used may be limited: this is not important, so long as those that are included are used naturally and provide a good model for learners.

Examples of spoken English, whether for dialogue work or listening, should be reasonably representative of natural spoken English, although again some simplification is to be expected. For example, the main conventions for conversation, such as turn-taking, should be respected. This aspect will be explored in more detail in Chapter 10 when we shall look at communicative coursebooks.

When coursebooks set out to teach aspects of discourse, it is most commonly in the area of writing. Here there may be material on organizing different kinds of written work, such as narratives, reports, letters, etc. The conventions of different formats may be explained – for example, how to set out a formal letter; and advice may be given on the ordering of events, ideas, etc.

At a more technical level, there may be examples and exercises on writing paragraphs, and on structuring a longer text into paragraphs. This is a difficult area, because there are no firm rules for paragraphing as there are for grammar. We are really dealing with how text is organized and how it is structured according to meaning and the development of a theme or an argument. Because there are no hard and fast rules, coursebooks tend to use a combination of explanation and advice supported by examples.

Another area of written English which often gets special attention is cohesion, and in particular conjunctions, or conjunctives as they are sometimes called. Some coursebooks use other names for them, such as sequencers or text organizers. Basically, they act as signalling devices or signposts and help readers and listeners to find their way through a piece of continuous discourse by relating sentences to one another and helping the reader or listener to predict what is coming next. For example, compare your predictions of how these two sequences might continue:

Howard is really a very nice person and ...
Howard is really a very nice person but ...

Conjunctives play an important role in effective communication. They operate both within sentences, joining clauses, and between sentences, linking but not joining them. The following example from *Highlight Upper Intermediate* shows how a coursebook deals with conjunctives in written discourse.

Relative clauses: *who, which, whose*   40

4 Put *who, which* or *whose* into each space.

This is the story of a strange event [a]_____ took place in England recently. A man [b]_____ brother had disappeared in France in 1944 received a letter from someone [c]_____ claimed to be Graham, his brother. The man, [d]_____ had given up hope of ever seeing his brother again, was overjoyed to receive the letter, [e]_____ was posted in France. He wrote back and received another letter [f]_____ gave the name and address of a French family, [g]_____, the letter said, had been looking after Graham. Graham's brother took the next plane to France, and soon arrived at the address [h]_____ his brother had given. The people [i]_____ lived there did not know his brother, and had not written any letters, but they were looking after the graves of soldiers [j]_____ had been killed there during the war.

Text organisers   1   17

5 Study the examples, and answer the question at the end of each one.

  a *Although journalists often exaggerate stories, they are not supposed to change the facts.*
    Do they exaggerate stories? Are they supposed to change the facts?

  b *Journalists do change the facts. However, they are not supposed to.*
    Does this have the same meaning as sentence **a**?

  c *Journalists often exaggerate stories. They are not supposed to, however.*
    Does this have the same meaning as sentence **a**?

  d *In spite of my advice, the journalist changed the story.*
    Did we advise the journalist to change the story?

  e *While journalists often exaggerate stories, they are supposed to give the facts.*
    Which of the underlined words in sentences **a, b, c, d** could be used instead of while?

  f *Journalists often record interviews. As well as this, they might keep written notes of what is said.*
    Is this phrase used to repeat information, or to add something new?

  g *Besides this* ...
    Can you use this phrase in **f**?

  h *Journalists lead quite an interesting life. On the other hand, they are not very well paid at the start of their careers.*
    Can you use this phrase in any other part of this exercise?

Text organisers

6 Complete the text by using words and phrases underlined in the examples in **5**.

There are many stories about the Bermuda Triangle, an area of ocean in the Caribbean, but [1]_____ many people believe that planes and ships mysteriously vanish there, there is no proof that this is true. [2]_____, it is true that many small boats disappear in the area. This is because it is an area of sudden bad weather, [3]_____, not because it is mysterious! One story describes how some planes disappeared there during the war, and [4]_____ this is true, the most likely explanation is that they ran out of fuel and crashed. [5]_____, there are stories suggesting that aliens may be responsible for the 'strange' disappearances. [6]_____ many investigations, no proof has ever been found that there is anything mysterious about the place at all!

98

From *Highlight Upper Intermediate*, Vince (Heinemann 1992)

Coursebooks are less likely to focus on the rules or conventions of spoken discourse, perhaps because it is a complex area and one that is only now becoming better understood, particularly through work being done in conversational analysis. However some materials do give attention to certain features of spoken discourse, pointing out, for example, how conversations start and how they end. *Cambridge Advanced English* (Jones 1991), for example, provides this schema for opening and closing conversations, linking it to a listening activity.

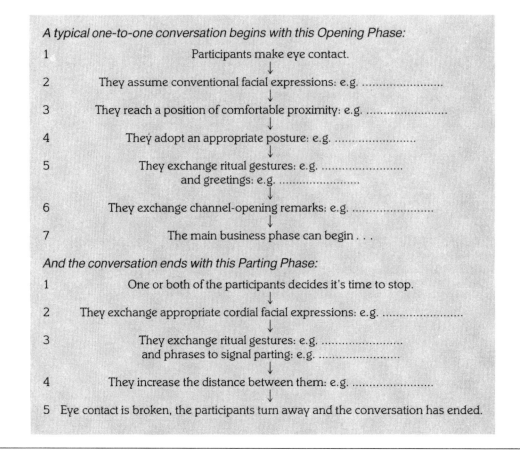

13.2   A 'typical' English conversation   Listening

A   Before you listen to the recording, look at the flowchart below and see if you can think of some examples to fill the gaps.

Listen to the recording and fill the gaps with some of the examples given by the speaker.

A typical one-to-one conversation begins with this Opening Phase:

1   Participants make eye contact.
       ↓
2   They assume conventional facial expressions: e.g. ....
       ↓
3   They reach a position of comfortable proximity: e.g. ....
       ↓
4   They adopt an appropriate posture: e.g. ....
       ↓
5   They exchange ritual gestures: e.g. ....
       and greetings: e.g. ....
       ↓
6   They exchange channel-opening remarks: e.g. ....
       ↓
7   The main business phase can begin . . .

And the conversation ends with this Parting Phase:

1   One or both of the participants decides it's time to stop.
       ↓
2   They exchange appropriate cordial facial expressions: e.g. ....
       ↓
3   They exchange ritual gestures: e.g. ....
       and phrases to signal parting: e.g. ....
       ↓
4   They increase the distance between them: e.g. ....
       ↓
5   Eye contact is broken, the participants turn away and the conversation has ended.

From *Cambridge Advanced English*, Jones (CUP 1991)

This is a useful guide and begins to sensitize learners to some of the ways in which conversations are structured and to some of the conventions that are brought into play.

At a lower level, the *Conversation Planner* in *Flying Colours 2* (Garton-Sprenger and Greenall 1991) is helpful in guiding learners through a straightforward conversation, although it does not deal with opening and closing strategies.

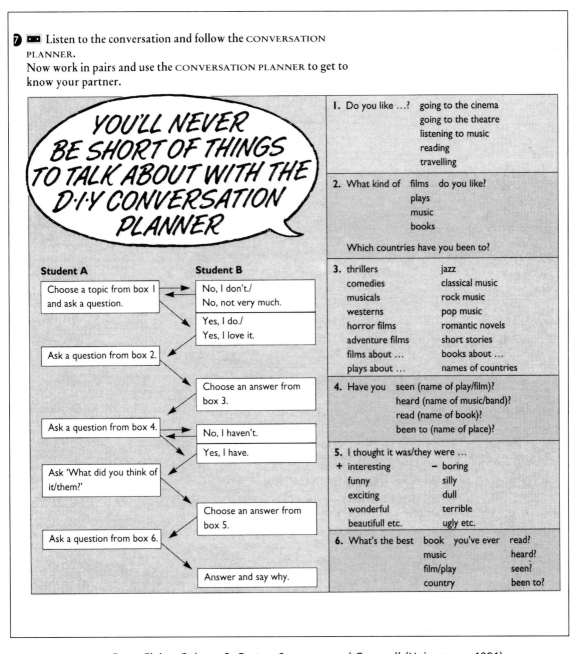

7 ▭ Listen to the conversation and follow the CONVERSATION PLANNER.
Now work in pairs and use the CONVERSATION PLANNER to get to know your partner.

From *Flying Colours 2*, Garton-Sprenger and Greenall (Heinemann 1991)

Checklist for discourse

- ☐ Does the coursebook deal with any aspects of discourse?
- ☐ If so, which aspects are covered:
  - conjunctives
  - other features of cohesion (reference pronouns, substitution, etc)
  - paragraphing and organization of written discourse
  - structure and conventions of spoken discourse?
- ☐ Do the examples of spoken and written discourse presented by the material provide good models for the learners?
- ☐ Is the treatment of discourse sustained and progressive throughout the course, or does it consist of limited or isolated elements?

8   Style and appropriacy

Language is very sensitive to its context of use and is stylistically variable. We should look at coursebooks from the angle of appropriacy to see how far they go in preparing learners to use appropriate styles in varying situations. Speakers make use of different styles of language to communicate in a way which complements the more literal meaning of words and sentences. For example, adopting an informal style of speech or writing is a statement about the relationship which exists between the people who are communicating with each other.

This awareness of the importance of appropriacy derives from the seminal work by Hymes (1971) on communicative competence, summed up in his now classic statement, 'There are rules of use without which the rules of grammar would be useless.' When we use language, we need to be able to perceive the social situations in which we are operating and to be able to match language style to situation.

For foreign learners, as for children acquiring their mother tongue, there is a double task: to perceive and understand the nature of the social situations they find themselves in and to select and use appropriate language. One aspect of the task is non-linguistic and the other is linguistic, but they are so closely connected that we cannot afford to neglect either of them. Language and culture are here seen to be closely intertwined.

Stylistic differences in English can be signalled by aspects of grammar, choice of vocabulary, discourse structure and aspects of phonology. In the area of grammar, use of the passive as opposed to the active form of verbs can be cited as an example of formal style. Another example is the use of contractions, such as *can't* and *won't* in writing, to signal informality. There are many examples of formal/non-formal distinctions in vocabulary, but one example will suffice: *ascend* and *go up* are virtually identical in terms of literal meaning, but are very different stylistically. Turning to discourse, the discourse structure of a formal speech is very different from that of a conversation between friends. Similarly, an informal letter is structured and set out differently from a business letter.

In the area of pronunciation, intonation can differ according to the degree of formality, as pointed out in *Headway Intermediate* Teacher's Book (Soars, J. and L. 1986):

Common problems

1 Intonation.
   Students sound too flat, start too low, and do not show a wide enough voice range. It is vital to point out that politeness is conveyed not by choice of exponent, but by intonation. In requests, students will need a lot of practice in starting high, showing a wide voice range, and rising slightly at the end.

Could you open the window, please?

Use the tapes as a model for intensive practice.

The more distant and formal the situation, the higher the start will be, and the greater the fall. Similarly, in a more familiar situation, the voice range will be narrower.

From *Headway Intermediate* Teacher's Book, Soars and Soars (OUP 1986)

Two examples of exercises focusing on the contrast between formal and informal style, with particular reference to vocabulary, are shown below and at the top of p 52.

7 Which of these phrases would you *not* expect to see in a personal letter?

All the best.
I refer to your letter of the 19th March.
It was so nice to hear from you.
I'm sure it'll be OK.

I am grateful for your assistance.
Look forward to seeing you!
I apologise for the delay in replying.
When are you coming up?

8 Rewrite the formal phrases in Exercise 7 in a less formal way.

From *Intermediate Matters*, Bell and Gower (Longman 1991)

---

5 Match the expressions in the list
below which are similar in
meaning.

enclose   job   currently
any more you need to know
now   occupation
any further information you
require
I can come   consider
the story of my life   look at
date of birth   curriculum vitae
I am available   aim to achieve
health   birthday   put in
medical history   hope to pass

Say which are formal and which
are informal

From *Vista*, Deller and Jones (Heinemann 1992)

Checklist for appropriacy

- ☐ Is there any reference to appropriacy?
- ☐ If so, is it dealt with thoroughly or incidentally?
- ☐ Is appropriacy taught with reference to:
  - – choice of grammar
  - – choice of vocabulary
  - – discourse structure
  - – pronunciation?
- ☐ Is there any attempt to match language style to social situation?
- ☐ Does the coursebook identify situations or areas of language use where learners should be particularly sensitive to using appropriate styles, eg when complaining?

9   Varieties of English

In addition to formal and informal distinctions, we need to consider which varieties of English are contained in the coursebook. Geographically speaking, there are two main varieties of English in the world, British English and American English. The standard forms of these two varieties differ to a small extent in grammar and vocabulary, and rather more in pronunciation. Nevertheless, they are mutually intelligible and demonstrably the same language. There are of course many different regional varieties of British and American English, and the further they diverge from the standard variety, the less intelligible they may become to outsiders. There are also many other varieties of English throughout the world, some used by native speakers, such as Irish and Australian English, others spoken mainly as a second language, as is the case of English in India and Singapore.

We also need to consider the increasingly common phenomenon of 'international English'. This concept refers to the use of English as a *lingua franca* around the world for business people, scientists and many others of diverse nationalities and mother tongues. Course materials such as *International Issues* (Potter 1991) are now on the market to meet the demand for international English.

Generally speaking, coursebooks for general use in several different countries take either standard southern British English – but not the traditional received pronunciation (RP) – or standard American English as their model. International English is usually based on one or other of these two varieties.

Courses produced for use in individual countries where English has the role of a second language will normally take the local variety as their model, but without features which are considered to be colloquial or non-standard.

Checklist for varieties of English

☐ Which geographical variety of English is taught:
  – British
  – American
  – other
  – international English?
☐ Whichever variety is taught, is there reference to other varieties (eg in a British English course, is there reference to American English where it differs)?

Conclusion

Analysing coursebooks for their language content is complex and multi-dimensional. In most situations you will have to decide on your priorities and focus on them. One typical scenario is the following: at elementary level, grammatical form and pronunciation will be the main priorities; at intermediate level, more attention will be focused on the appropriate use of grammatical structures, on vocabulary development and on aspects of stress and intonation; at advanced level, discourse structure and appropriacy will be added to the agenda.

This of course is only an example and you might like to think about what your priority areas are for analysing the language contained in coursebooks, relating your decisions to your aims and objectives and to your teaching situation.

Chapter 5 Selection and grading

Coursebook writers are in effect designing a syllabus as well as producing teaching material, and implicit in coursebooks for language learning there must be a view of and an approach to syllabus design. We need to know on what basis the content of the coursebook has been selected and how the content has been graded.

1 The syllabus base

Any coursebook will be permeated with the writer's assumptions about syllabus design, whether they have been explicitly formulated and theoretically justified or not. So it is very important that, when analysing and evaluating this aspect of materials, we should be aware of the options that are available to coursebook writers when they design their syllabuses.

A syllabus can be broadly defined as a specification of the work to be covered over a period of time, with a starting point and a final goal. The language content will be ordered in some way, usually being sequenced according to underlying principles or theories. In some cases the amount of time to be spent on each section will be specified. The focus of a syllabus, therefore, is on *what* is taught and *in what order* it is taught. There is a strong implication that what is taught is also learned, and both selection and sequencing of content will aim to facilitate learning. The mainstream concept of the syllabus has little more to say about the learning processes involved and does not specify the approach to teaching or the methods to be employed.

However, some alternative views of syllabus design, notably the **process syllabus**, are based on the learning process rather than on the content. The process syllabus is somewhat experimental in nature and has yet to make an impact on the bulk of teaching materials. The content is not specified in advance and there are no predetermined goals. The process syllabus grows naturally out of the learning situation and to some extent is set out retrospectively as the situation evolves. There is considerable scope for on-going negotiation among learners and between learners and teachers as the direction of a particular course develops. The emphasis is on process rather than product, on how learning develops naturally rather than on the prior selection and sequencing of what is to be taught.

As coursebooks are themselves products and their writers of necessity have to decide in advance what they are going to contain, there is a marked predominance in published materials of the **content-based syllabus**. There are however some examples of course material designed to allow for flexibility of use and deliberately avoiding a predetermined start and finish. Among the titles which are designed for selective use of this kind are the Macmillan *Dossiers* series (1991) and *The Sourcebook* (Shepherd and Cox 1991), which claims specifically that it gives users

the freedom to plan their teaching and learning, and an opportunity to negotiate *their* syllabus. They can:

- construct tailor-made programmes of learning according to student need;
- use the book in class or for self-access;
- use the book on courses of different length, ie year-round programmes, 12-week intensive courses and short courses.

Such books act as useful resources and are invaluable to teachers and learners alike when they choose to negotiate a syllabus. Nevertheless the books themselves do not participate in the elaboration and development of the process syllabus, and their content is still predetermined, even if the sequencing is not.

2   Content-based syllabuses

White (1988) identifies four types of content base in syllabus design. These are:

- form (with a structural focus)
- function (with a notional/functional basis)
- situation (with a contextual focus)
- topic (with an informational focus).

I will identify the main characteristics of each of these syllabus bases, but it should be borne in mind that the actual content of coursebooks will be based on a combination of these factors. Coursebook writers have to balance the competing demands of different approaches to syllabus design and produce a version which is best suited to the users' needs.

3   Structural and functional syllabuses

The **structural syllabus** incorporates probably the most traditional approach and is based on the internal structure of the language with particular emphasis on grammatical structure. Lexis and possibly phonology will also be taken into account, but the foundation of the structural syllabus is grammar. The selection and sequencing of language items in a structural syllabus is based on no firm theory or principle, but is determined by writers in a pragmatic fashion with reliance on established orthodoxy and practical experience. The general guidelines used in the case of grammar items tend to be:

- complexity of structure
- 'learnability'
- usefulness.

Clearly complexity and learnability appear to be connected, in that more complex structures are more difficult to learn. So, for example, the past perfect continuous is considered to be more difficult to learn than the present simple because it is more complex in structure. Another factor affecting learnability is the use, or underlying meaning of grammatical forms. I have referred in an earlier chapter to the difficulty experienced by many learners in understanding the uses of the present perfect and the meanings of articles, especially where there are not similar forms in the learner's native language. The form of the present perfect and of articles in English is not complex, but their use can give rise to difficulty because of the relatively difficult meaning concepts involved.

Usefulness as a concept for selection of language items is relatively subjective unless a detailed needs analysis has been undertaken with a clearly specified group of learners, and this is not the case with mass-produced coursebooks. There is, however, a pragmatic perception among coursebook writers of what is more useful at the early stages of a course. Coverage is a major criterion affecting usefulness, so the present continuous, allowing the learner to talk about the immediate present, the immediate future, intentions, etc provides a rich return for a relatively small investment in learning effort. It is not surprising therefore that this item usually occurs early on in a course and is given prominence.

By contrast, the complicated tense changes required for reported speech require a good deal more learning and internalization if they are to be used quickly and fluently, and have less immediate usefulness to the learner in the early stages of learning. Moreover a considerable amount of prior knowledge of verb forms and uses is required before students can begin to approach this area of English. So it is not surprising that it usually occurs much later in a course.

In the case of coursebooks which are designed for speakers of the same mother tongue, differences between the structure of English and of the native language will provide a further guide for selection. Contrastive analysis can be a useful tool for predicting and explaining ease and difficulty of learning different items and it would almost certainly exert an influence, formally or informally, on syllabus design for monolingual groups.

The strength of a structural syllabus is that it can account for all the forms of a language and relate them to one another in a coherent way. A serious limitation of a purely structural syllabus, on the other hand, would be the scant regard paid to meaning, and especially to the communicative potential of what is taught.

The **functional syllabus** is based on the identification of communicative functions and owes its development to work done under the aegis of the Council of Europe in the early 1970s. The notional/functional principles of syllabus design underlying the functional syllabus-base are set out in *Notional Syllabuses* (Wilkins 1976). They had a significant impact on coursebook design and led to several courses published in the late 1970s and early 1980s which used language functions extensively in selecting and organizing language content.

In this approach to syllabus design, communicative functions are selected and sequenced according to usefulness to the learner, the extent to which they meet the learner's communicative needs. So, the earliest items on the syllabus will be those that learners will need most in the situations in which they will use English. Predicting those situations in all but the most general way for the purposes of producing coursebooks for widespread use is problematic. As in the case of the structural syllabus, there is no straightforward mechanism for doing it, and, in general, syllabus designers and coursebook writers rely on a pragmatic approach, combining experience, intuition and common sense. Ultimately the choices are to a considerable extent subjective.

An advantage of a functional base to coursebook design is that the learning goals can be identified in terms which make sense to the learners themselves. To the average student, 'making requests for information' means more than 'interrogative form of modal verbs followed by infinitive'. Another advantage is that the coursebook writer can ensure that the learning process has an immediate practical result in that the students can use what they have learned outside the classroom at a relatively early stage. Students who do not complete a course will still be able to take away with them something useful in the form of a limited communicative ability in English.

However, unlike grammar, functions do not form an interrelated finite system, nor have they been fully and comprehensively described. Most lists of functions so far produced have been very selective, and it is not at all clear just what a complete account of communicative functions would consist of, even assuming that it were feasible to produce such an account.

Widdowson (1979) has pointed out that a functional syllabus, like a structural syllabus, is an inventory of units and that is why I have grouped them together as content-based syllabuses. Neither of them can fully account for communicative competence because they do not contain the strategies necessary for using linguistic elements for communicative purposes. Such strategies amount to more than just combining communicative functions learned in isolation and include 'an ability to *make* (create) sense as a participant in discourse ... by the skilful deployment of shared knowledge of ... language resources and rules of language use' (Widdowson 1979). This is the realm of pragmatics, a territory barely explored yet by most coursebooks.

Structural and functional syllabuses are not opposed to each other, as they have sometimes been seen to be, but are complementary. The functional perspective of a functional syllabus develops the structural syllabus by incorporating into it a component which is sensitive to the learners' communicative needs and provides them with units of communication as well as units of language form. Furthermore, syllabuses of this multi-dimensional kind must establish links between form and function, showing how communicative functions are realized through language form.

4 Situational and topic-based syllabuses

The **situational syllabus** takes 'real-world' situations as an organizing principle in selecting and grading what is to be taught. The factors that come into play are:

- participants
- setting
- communicative goals.

From such an initial analysis, the materials writer will produce contextualized examples and exercises that will present relevant instances of language and provide contexts for it to be practised in. Grammar, vocabulary, etc derive from the situations selected and are not themselves the driving force behind selection. However, concepts of complexity of structure, learnability, etc must come into play when language exponents are being selected, as there will inevitably be many different ways of using language in the same situational encounter.

The situations selected will usually be of a relatively restricted nature, usually involving some kind of practical transaction, such as booking in at a hotel, or using a garage, and the language taught will also tend to be somewhat restricted. It is difficult to produce a situationally-based syllabus which also deals systematically with grammar, so that the learners are genuinely learning the structure of the language in a way which will allow them to use it subsequently in situations completely different from those presented in the coursebook.

A situationally-based syllabus comes somewhere between the phrase book and full language learning. Its limitation lies in being too closely tied to the specific situations that it selects and in the difficulty of ensuring that the structure of the language is adequately covered. Nevertheless situational considerations, along with the others referred to in this chapter, will be taken into account by most syllabus designers and coursebook writers, even though they will probably not be the main force in determining content or sequencing.

Topic-based syllabuses take information content as the main principle for selecting and organizing the syllabus content. It is unlikely that the syllabuses of general English courses will be wholly topic-based, as the concept of the topic is too imprecise and difficult to define. However, like situation, topic may be a secondary factor in determining syllabus content and the various topics that are included in the course will figure in the schema of a multi-dimensional syllabus. Indeed several coursebooks have a column in their contents maps showing which topics are included and where, as it is felt important that interesting and stimulating topics should be part of the overall content of the course.

Topic can be of great value in keeping learners' interest and maintaining or increasing their motivation. Additionally, it provides a focus for the language input contained in the course and helps to create a sense of coherence within individual units.

There is also evidence that some students may learn better when they are focusing on content material presented through English, rather than focusing on the language itself. Certainly this is the situation pertaining in schools where English is the medium of instruction but a foreign or second language for the students. High standards of English are often achieved in such schools. Consequently, the inclusion of well-chosen topic-based material in some quantity can improve learner performance. The inclusion of literature in some courses is another example of shifting the focus from the language to topic-based content.

Two of the stated principles behind *Connect* (Revell 1990), a course designed for students at upper secondary level, emphasize the importance attached to topic and subject content:

> Students should be able to **learn about other things** as they learn English: English should be linked to other subjects in the school curriculum and to the world outside the school.
> A coursebook should provide **interesting content**: it should be challenging and appropriate for the age group, and not offer childish content just because the learners' language skills are low.

Checklist for selection of content

☐ To what extent is the content selected according to:
  – structure
  – functions
  – situations
  – topics?
☐ Is any one of the above predominant as the basis of selection of content?
☐ How well does the coursebook balance the above factors in selecting content and to what extent is it successful in integrating the different approaches?
☐ Is any of the material suitable for use as a resource in a negotiated (process) syllabus?

5   Grading: sequencing and staging

Grading refers to the way in which the content is organized in the syllabus or coursebook, involving the ordering of items and the speed with which the students progress through the course. A useful distinction has been made between **sequencing** and **staging**.

Sequencing refers to the order in which new items are taught, how the components fit with one another and how the range of language taught develops as learners progress through the course. Implicit in sequencing is the concept of progression, with the expectation that there will be a principled development from a beginning point to an end point. Although sequencing is inherent to a syllabus and to most coursebooks, there are few recognized principles for the guidance of writers, beyond the pragmatic considerations referred to earlier in this chapter.

However, there is a substantial degree of similarity in the way structural syllabuses are sequenced, as writers draw on the cumulative experience of language teachers and the feedback received from learners. Based on this, a tradition has grown up in which some language items are clearly perceived as being more complex, more difficult to learn or less useful than others. As we shall see later in this chapter, competing coursebooks sequence their material, at least in the early stages of learning, with remarkable similarity.

Within the sequencing of material, **recycling** is an important consideration. It is rarely sufficient to present and practise a language item once only and then consider it dealt with. Learners need to meet items on several occasions, and preferably in different contexts, in order to fix them in memory, gain fluency in using them and come to a full understanding of their meanings. We therefore need to check that new items are recycled sufficiently frequently in the course. This applies to grammar and particularly to vocabulary items. By the nature of things, grammar items are likely to turn up again (although we would of course like to see this happen in a planned way), but vocabulary items, except the commonest words, could very well occur once or twice and then disappear without trace unless the coursebook writers are very careful to recycle them.

Staging refers to the way a course is divided into units, how much material each unit contains, the speed of progression and the size of the learning load. Staging is to some extent a function of the time spent in learning and the amount learned. So it concerns how much new material is introduced in a given number of hours, how close together or how far apart new grammar items are in relation to one another, how much new vocabulary is introduced in each unit, and so on. A steeply staged course might introduce a substantial new grammar item in each unit. For example:

Unit 4 present continuous
Unit 5 *shall/will* future
Unit 6 past simple
Unit 7 present perfect

Supposing there were four or five practice activities in each unit, and a short reading or listening passage with between twenty and thirty new vocabulary items, then the material would be considered to be steeply graded, assuming about six hours' work in class for each unit. Such a course would most probably not be intended for students learning these items for the first time, but rather for false beginners.

A course with shallow staging, to take an example at the other extreme, would be one which devoted four units to the verb *to be* in the present tense and introduced between ten and fifteen new words per unit, following with another four units devoted to the present continuous with its immediate present meaning. With such shallow staging, we would expect very thorough presentation and extensive practice, together with a good deal of skills work involving reading and listening as well as spoken skills and some carefully guided writing. There would also be time for some detailed work on pronunciation. Such a course would be suitable for beginners who had had no previous contact with English and who were experiencing difficulty in making fast progress, perhaps because they were being taught in large classes or because there were large differences between their native language (L1) and English, including perhaps the use of a different writing system.

We should also check whether the coursebook has a linear or cyclical progression. A course with linear progression adopts an order of presentation which deals with each language item exhaustively before passing on to the next item. A cyclical progression moves fairly quickly from one language item to another, and then progressively returns to each item, maybe on several occasions, later in the course. The effect of this is that the learners acquire a wider range of practical competence in the language early on, but have not learned each language item as thoroughly as in a linear course. When deciding between a linear or cyclical progression, we need to be aware of the individual and cultural preferences of the learners, the length of the course, its goals and whether the students will follow the course to its end.

Checklist for grading

- ☐ Is there any evident basis for the sequencing of the content?
- ☐ If so, is it structural? Is the sequencing based on complexity, learnability, usefulness, etc?
- ☐ Is there any other basis for sequencing – eg functional organization, situational organization, organization according to topic?
- ☐ If several influences come to play on the sequencing, how well are they balanced?
- ☐ Are new language items adequately recycled?
- ☐ Is the staging of the language content
  - – shallow
  - – average
  - – steep?
- ☐ Are the staging and sequencing suitable for the learners?
- ☐ Is the progression of the course
  - – linear
  - – cyclical?

6 Case study: selection and grading

A review of the main general English courses on the market at the time of writing shows that only a proportion of them discuss in their teachers' books how the content has been selected. In most of the cases where selection is discussed, it is in a largely descriptive way, identifying which criteria have been used, but giving little or no information on the principles underlying the selection, ie *why* the stated criteria have been used, or *how* they have been applied.

One of the most detailed statements on the content of the course is made by *The New Cambridge English Course* (Swan and Walter 1990). Referring to its 'multi-syllabus course design', the authors state that 'a complete English language course will incorporate at least eight main syllabuses' which they list as:

vocabulary
grammar
pronunciation
notions
functions
situations
topics
skills

The authors of *Flying Colours* (Garton-Sprenger and Greenall 1991) state that:

The syllabuses covered include functions, notions, structures, topics, lexis, skills, phonology and learner training.

The teacher's book of *New Dimensions* (Lonergan and Gordon 1986) tells us that:

The syllabus of **New Dimensions** is multi-dimensional – aiming to reconcile and unify different (and sometimes conflicting) types of syllabus. The syllabus dimensions that are woven together in **New Dimensions** systematically develop the students' ability to *do* things through English (functions), to express ideas in English (notions), to know about grammatical forms and patterns (structures), to be aware of different uses of English in different situations and on different topics (situations/topics), to master a wide and useful English vocabulary (lexis), to speak English with accurate pronunciation, natural rhythm and intonation (phonology), and to listen to, speak, read and write English efficiently (language skills).

Other courses make less detailed statements, such as *Grapevine* (Viney, P. and K. 1990), which refers to:

A clear, carefully-ordered syllabus
The syllabus has interwoven structural and functional elements. They have been designed to follow a clear and logical progression. We have tried to balance the immediate communicative needs with the long-term aims of knowledge of the grammatical system.

And in some cases there is no explicit reference to syllabus design at all. This does not, of course, necessarily mean that such courses do not have a carefully considered content. It may simply be that the writers have not thought it appropriate to discuss their criteria with the course users. In this case the materials evaluator's task is more difficult as it is necessary to work backwards from the materials in order to work out what selection criteria were probably used.

The examples of coursebook syllabuses given above show a remarkable degree of similarity. In fact two are identical (*The New Cambridge English Course* and *New Dimensions*), whilst *Flying Colours* differs only in including 'learner training' and leaving out 'situation'.

The contents pages or contents maps of other courses include some, but not all of the dimensions referred to above. For example *Highlight* (Vince 1992) includes:

> language (grammar)
> activities (notions/functions and communicative activities)
> skills
> vocabulary
> phonology

Intermediate Matters (Bell and Gower 1991) includes the following headings in its 'contents chart':

> topics
> grammar/functions
> vocabulary
> pronunciation
> writing

It also makes more general reference to reading, listening and speaking and to learning strategies.

Whilst some coursebooks are more forthcoming than others about the selection of content, none amongst those that I have surveyed have much to say about the principles guiding the grading (sequencing and staging) of the material. A number of courses tell us that the different strands of the syllabus are carefully interwoven and that different types of syllabus are reconciled to provide a degree of unity in the material. However, there is little insight given into how this is done and according to what principles. This underlines our earlier discovery that there is little available to materials writers in terms of elaborated theory or principle when it comes to grading. Empirical evidence is sparse, and in any case difficult to apply, and insights gained from language acquisition research may not be applicable in whole or in part to foreign or second language learning situations. Consequently in the time-honoured tradition of language teaching, coursebook writers will rely on a pragmatic approach which is based on professional experience, insights into learning processes, a feeling for what is possible and a general awareness of what works.

Illustrative of statements on grading to be found in teachers' books are the following:

> All the language items in the course are presented in an order which meets the most urgent requirements of survival English.
> *Flying Colours*

> The priorities given to these different dimensions of the syllabus vary from one part of a unit to another, and from one part of the course to another depending on the demands of the themes or language areas, or on the likely demands of the students at particular points in the course.
> *New Dimensions*

> They [structural and functional elements] have been designed to follow a clear and logical progression.
> *Grapevine*

Conclusion

Clearly the whole area of syllabus design and the selection and grading of content in coursebooks is complex and multi-dimensional. The coursebook writer has a difficult job in developing material whilst attempting to balance and reconcile some eight criteria for selection and grading, some of them potentially in conflict. There is a relatively sophisticated awareness of the need for balance between the different criteria in syllabus design and a sensitivity to the need for as integrated an approach as possible. A major task of the coursebook writer is to accommodate different kinds of syllabuses within the entity of the language course.

It does seem clear from an examination of the major courses available that they go a long way towards achieving a balance and accommodating the different dimensions of the syllabus. If there is a basic or core dimension, however, in the majority of cases it is the structural, or grammatical, syllabus. There is a long tradition of using structural syllabuses in language teaching, although it seemed that they might be overthrown by functional syllabuses in the late 1970s and early 1980s. However they have shown their strength by maintaining their primacy, and in the process have been enriched by the addition of the other dimensions of syllabus design that we have been looking at.

Chapter 6 **Skills**

1   The four skills in general coursebooks

How do coursebooks deal with the four skills (listening, speaking, reading and writing) which are seen as central to language learning? The skills dimension complements the dimension of grammatical/lexical/phonological knowledge and focuses on the ability of learners actually to operate in the language. The emphasis is on linguistic behaviour and on learners' ability to use the language in different situations requiring different skills, sometimes in isolation but more usually together.

We need to check if the coursebook deals adequately with all four skills, taking the level and overall aims into account, and if there is a suitable balance between the skills. We might note here that in-depth and balanced treatment of all four skills is not necessary for all teaching situations. Extensive reading, for example, would not be desirable in a coursebook designed to be used by native-speaker teachers in Japan, who would want the emphasis to be on listening and speaking.

Clearly the knowledge base of grammar, lexis, etc and the skills base of listening, speaking, etc must go hand-in-hand and coursebooks should develop students' skills in using English every bit as much as they help to develop students' knowledge (explicit or not) of the system of English.

So, as the grammar element in the course progresses and the vocabulary becomes more extensive, we should expect to see the skills work become more demanding. Dialogue work might become more complex, moving away from simple question-and-answer sequences. Similarly, listening passages would become longer, and might be spoken more quickly or with a slightly non-standard accent. Reading texts would also become longer, and the discourse structure more complex. Comprehension questions, which in the early stages of learning would check understanding of simple facts, might, as the course progresses, require learners to infer meaning, or to extract certain relevant information from a mass of less relevant information.

As an example of how skills work can progress, compare the two examples of dialogue work from *New Dimensions 1* (Lonergan and Gordon 1986) and *New Dimensions 3* (Ward and Lonergan 1988). The lower-level activity is a straightforward dialogue which follows a very predictable question–answer sequence – in fact there are six in the dialogue – and is consequently relatively easy for elementary-level learners to follow and repeat.

In comparison the example on p 66 from Book 3 of the course requires more complex skills, including the ability to restructure a piece of discourse from jumbled parts, to work through it as an oral exercise with a partner and to express the same ideas in written form as a formal report.

Read, listen and complete

Mary: Are you in a team?
Sam: Yes, I'm in the badminton team.
Mary: Are you very good?
Sam: Well, I can play quite well. Can you play badminton?
Mary: No, not very well. I'm a beginner. But I can play table tennis.
Sam: Can you? I like table tennis. How about a game at the sports centre on Saturday?
Mary: OK, but I can play very well. I'm in the team.
Sam: I can play quite well, don't worry. By the way, do you like dancing?
Mary: Yes, a lot. Why?
Sam: Well, there's a disco at the sports centre on Saturday evening . . .

Write in the names *Sam* or *Mary*.

Who . . .?	is in the team	can play very well	can play quite well	can't play very well	can't play
badminton					
table tennis					

From *New Dimensions 1*, Lonergan and Gordon (Macmillan 1986)

Despite the differences in complexity of operation required from the learners, both examples here include, directly or indirectly, practice in using all four skills in an integrated way, around the same topic. If we take writing as an example, we can see that in the elementary activity students are only expected to write in two names in the grid, *Sam* or *Mary*, and the purpose of this is mainly to check listening comprehension. Nevertheless, students are beginning to write in English in conjunction with other skills development. The writing activity in Book 3 is far more demanding and requires not only grammatical, lexical and orthographic knowledge, but also an ability to handle the style and conventions of formal writing, in this case report writing. Again, as in the example from Book 1, the writing activity develops naturally from other skills work, equipping learners not only with individual skills but also, and very importantly, with the ability to use language skills in association with one another, as happens in authentic discourse. The integration of skills is an important aspect of overall language ability and I often think in terms of a fifth skill: being able to integrate some or all of the other four skills in ways which are appropriate to the situation. This concept is central to the idea of communicative language teaching and will be developed further in Chapter 10, *Communicative coursebooks*.

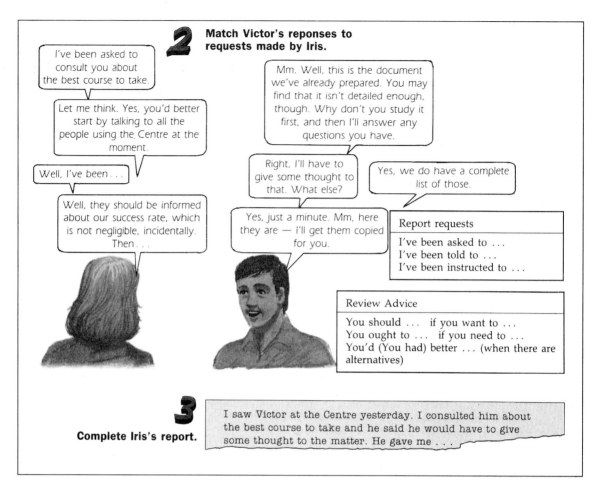

From *New Dimensions 3*, Ward and Lonergan (Macmillan 1988)

A further consideration is whether the material presented for skills work is specially written for the coursebook, is semi-authentic (originally authentic but simplified) or authentic. There is a school of thought that says that authentic materials can be used even at elementary level, so long as the questions, activities, etc based on them are suitably graded. Others would argue that for beginners, and beyond, the range of suitable authentic materials is very limited and tends to be rather trivial in nature, such as shopping lists and street signs. In practice, elementary-level material is usually specially written for the coursebook.

We should look for the use of authentic or semi-authentic material at an appropriate point in the coursebook, as it brings greater realism and relevance and can increase learner motivation. With authentic or nearly authentic material, we can be confident that the models of language being presented are genuine, particularly in terms of discourse structure, a feature which is sometimes difficult to replicate convincingly when writing specially for a coursebook. One principle holds for skills work: the examples of language presented and practised, whether authentic or not, should be good models for learning purposes and should be representative of real-life language use.

Checklist for skills

- ☐ Is practice in all four skills included?
- ☐ If so, is it balanced?
- ☐ If not, which skills are omitted, and why?
- ☐ Does the skills work progress in terms of complexity and difficulty, in line with the grammatical and lexical progression of the course? How well is this achieved?
- ☐ Do the presentation and practice activities include the integration of skills in realistic contexts? All four skills do not necessarily have to figure in every sequence of activities for it to be valid.
- ☐ Does the coursebook use authentic material at an appropriate level (eg pre-intermediate, intermediate, advanced)?
- ☐ If semi-authentic material is used, is it representative of authentic discourse?
- ☐ If non-authentic material is used, is it nevertheless a good model for learners to follow?

2 Listening

Coursebooks focus on listening in two different ways. Firstly as part of general oral work, including dialogues and roleplay, where listening plays a secondary role compared with speaking. One of the most difficult and often unnerving aspects of taking part in a conversation in a foreign language is the unpredictability of the answer or response. Whilst learners can keep what they try to say within their linguistic competence, there is no way that, once outside the safe confines of the classroom, they can control what comes back at them in conversation. The most effective strategy is quick thinking and accurate prediction of what to expect.

Coursebooks could do more here to help learners to cope with this problem, for example by providing dialogues where what the student says is well controlled and graded, but where the response is more difficult and harder to understand. Students could then be encouraged to develop strategies for coping, which would range from making informed guesses based on partial comprehension to asking for a repetition, which may or may not come in a simpler form, but would at least give extra thinking time.

The second way in which coursebooks handle listening is in its own right, with recorded listening passages for comprehension, for extraction of information, as a lead-in to discussion, in conjunction with a reading text, etc. We should check if the coursebook provides pre-listening activities to focus learners' attention on the topic of the passage. These can take the form of pre-questions, or asking students to look for certain items of information contained in the listening material. This gives purpose to the activity, allows an element of prediction and makes the passage more accessible by placing it in a context.

We also need to check the quality of the recorded sound. This should be very high. The speed of speaking should be appropriate to the learners' ability and level, and where different accents are used, they should not normally deviate too drastically from whichever (standard) variety the students have become used to from their teacher and previous listening. On the other hand, over-articulated speech is to be avoided and the models presented should include features such as elision, weak forms, assimilation, etc.

The kind of listening that I have just described is fairly universal in coursebooks and is a necessary part of skills development. However, it is perhaps not as realistic an activity as we might think because the listener is almost always overhearing something that he or she takes no part in and cannot influence in any way. It is like being the proverbial fly on the wall. In these circumstances it is usually impossible to understand much of what is being said because of elliptical references to items of shared information that the outside listener has no knowledge of. We often underestimate the difficulty our students experience in listening to such material, and we should expect the coursebook to give as much background information as possible to make comprehension easier.

Another factor contributing to the difficulty of understanding recorded material is the absence of vision, depriving students of all the supporting features normally available through facial expression, gesture, eye contact, etc. Videotapes can overcome this disadvantage if they are available, but the cost of purchasing the videotapes themselves and the equipment needed to play them means that at present there are far more audiotapes produced as part of course packages than videotapes, although videos are available as optional extras with some courses.

Checklist for listening

☐ What kind of listening material is contained in the course?
  – Does listening form part of dialogue/conversation work?
  – Are there specific listening passages?
☐ If there are specific listening passages, what kind of activities are based on them – comprehension questions, extracting specific information, etc?
☐ Is the listening material set in a meaningful context?
☐ Are there pre-listening tasks, questions, etc?
☐ What is the recorded material on audio-cassette like in terms of:
  – sound quality
  – speed of delivery
  – accent
  – authenticity?
☐ Is there any video material for listening?
☐ If so, is good use made of the visual medium to provide a meaningful context and show facial expression, gesture, etc?

3 Speaking

Few courses treat speaking as a separate skill in the same way as listening, reading and writing. Speaking practice takes place through the oral presentation and practice of new language items, in dialogue work and in roleplay, as mentioned above. The more mechanical aspects of speaking are also covered in pronunciation practice, where this forms part of the course package, and these elements combined normally ensure that students receive good spoken models from their teachers and ample opportunity to practise themselves.

Coursebooks vary in the amount of preparation they give at more advanced levels. Some simply provide topics for discussion, whilst others set up more realistic interactions through the use of communication activities, such as those to be found in *Cambridge Advanced English* (Jones 1991). The following is an example of the technique, which involves two students, each one looking at only one set of instructions (or cue card), which are on different pages in the back of the book.

B ☎ 💬 Work in pairs. One of you should look at Activity 35, the other at 59. You'll each see some notes: these are the points you have to communicate to your partner. Imagine that you're on the phone, and sit BACK-TO-BACK. Note down the information your partner gives you.

At the end of the call, compare your notes with the notes your partner was referring to (in 35 or 59).

—— 35 ——

Give this message to your partner over the phone. Note down the message your partner gives you.

- Your partner's meeting with Michael Steadman in Philadelphia put back - now at 9 a.m. on Tuesday 14th, not Monday afternoon.
- Pick up your airline ticket from TWA desk when you get to Heathrow.
- Your outward flight is TW 755 at 09.55 on 13 March, arriving 12.50
- Return on BA 218 at 20.50 on 15 March, arriving back at 08.45.
- Take only carry-on hand baggage.
- Go straight to his office at 143 4th Street in the morning.
- Phone him to confirm all this on 0101 215 777 5482.

—— 59 ——

Give this message to your partner over the phone. Note down the message your partner gives you.

- Your partner's meeting with Jane Potter on Tuesday 14 June rescheduled - train strike.
- Meet her 12.45 in foyer of Grosvenor Hotel.
- Please book table for three for 1.30 (Hilda Meyer will be joining you).
- In case of problems getting out of London, book hotel room for yourself for Tuesday night - not too expensive!
- Recommended hotel: Cambridge Arms, 135 Alexander St - near Victoria Station (phone 071 222 9826).
- Bring your latest sales figures and forecasts on 3½ inch IBM-compatible floppy disks - not hard copies.
- Contact Ms Potter on 081 345 8921 or Ms Meyer on 01049 567 93220.

From *Cambridge Advanced English*, Jones (CUP 1991)

This kind of activity includes an element of uncertainty and unpredictability, which is present in any genuine conversation or discussion but is lacking in many EFL coursebooks. By doing activities like this, students can gain confidence in participating in conversation whilst in the relative safety of the classroom and can develop strategies for coping with the unpredictability involved.

These useful activities replicate situations in which conversations take place by creating an information gap, but they do not actually *teach* how to organize conversation in English.

Two examples of material which aims to teach strategies and skills of speaking are shown on pp 71–2. They are from *Elementary Conversation* (Geddes and Sturtridge 1992) and *Advanced Conversation* (Geddes, Sturtridge and Been 1991). They focus on *saying what you mean* and on *getting around vocabulary difficulties* at elementary level, and on *learning how to redirect a conversation* at advanced level. Here we need to evaluate how effectively the material equips learners for real-life interactions.

Checklist for speaking

- ☐ How much emphasis is there on spoken English in the coursebook?
- ☐ What kind of material for speaking is contained in the course? This may include:
  - – oral presentation and practice of language items
  - – dialogues
  - – roleplay
  - – communication activities (information gap)
- ☐ Are there any specific strategies for conversation or other spoken activities, eg debating, giving talks?
- ☐ Is any practice material included to help learners to cope with unpredictability in spoken discourse?

PART ONE

UNIT FIVE

EXPLAINING WHAT YOU MEAN

Phrase Box

Saying you don't know a word	I'm not sure of	the word (in English).
	I don't know	the English for...
		what it's called in English.
	What do you call it in English?	
Describing	It's like a ...	It's a ｜ sort ｜ of ...
	It's made of ...	｜ kind ｜
	It's a thing ｜ for (washing dishes)	
	It's stuff ｜ to (wash dishes)	
	｜ you use to (wash dishes)	
	It's used ｜ for ... (v + ing)	
	You use it ｜ to ... (v)	
	It's a ｜ place where ...	
	｜ thing which/that ...	
	｜ person who ...	
Using 'family' words	a mug → a big cup	
	a boat	
	a barge ｝ → a small ship	
	a yacht	
Helping	You mean ...	

Developing skills

Task 1

Work in pairs. **A** and **B** are doing an English vocabulary exercise. Read their conversation by matching the phrases.

A

– What do you call a thing which shows the months of the year?

– A puppy. I don't know the English for a thing you use for cooking.

– Gloves. What's the English for a place where children like to go – where they go and play?

– That's right.

B

– That's easy. A playground. I want the word for a small dog.

– Do you mean a saucepan?

– You mean a calendar. I don't know the English for things you put on your hands when it's cold.

28

From *Elementary Conversation*, Geddes and Sturtridge (Macmillan 1992)

1.2 Redirecting the conversation

1.2   Task 1

To redirect a conversation, you can often pick up a word or phrase that has just been used and say:

> *Talking of ....*
> *Speaking ....*
> *Talking of X makes me think of ....*
> *That reminds me. That reminds me of ....*
> *Incidentally ....*

For example:

A   I went with Rachel to that new Indian **restaurant** on Sunday. It was her birthday.

B   (*encouraging*) Really? (*redirecting*) **That reminds me**, did you know that a very good Sri Lankan **restaurant** has just opened in my neighbourhood?

or: **Incidentally**, I've just come back from Scotland. You can find Chinese **restaurants** all over the place there.

or: **Talking of eating**, did you know that people in Papua New Guinea eat ants? I was reading about it last night.

A   (*encouraging*) How interesting.

From *Advanced Conversation*, Geddes, Sturtridge and Been (Macmillan 1991)

4 Reading

Reading is the one activity that can be done easily and without any equipment by students outside the classroom. All they need is access to suitable texts and reference material, such as a dictionary or wordlist. This can be provided easily by the coursebook and most include reading passages from early on at elementary level.

Reading texts can be used for several different purposes, and this is reflected in coursebooks:

- developing reading skills and strategies
- presenting/recycling grammar items
- extending vocabulary
- providing models for writing
- giving information of interest to students
- stimulating oral work.

Reading texts also allow students to reflect on the structure and use of language at their own pace without the sometimes stressful real-time constraints that go with listening and speaking. This is an essential characteristic of reading as an activity: the reader is in control of the pace and this is an important consideration for foreign-language learners.

We should check if reading passages in the coursebook are:

- of real interest
- as authentic as possible considering the level
- well presented and accompanied by purposeful activities which help the reading process.

Reading can be linked to other skills work, particularly listening and writing. Some coursebooks have reading texts recorded on cassette and ask learners to listen as they read. The advantages of this include linking written English to its pronunciation, providing models for stress and intonation and generally bringing the text to life. Corresponding disadvantages are that learners are unable to set their own pace, at least at the first reading, and that they may be encouraged to vocalize or sub-vocalize when reading, a habit which, if continued at more advanced levels, would reduce reading speed.

When the reading text, or part of it, is used as a model for written work, learners are usually asked to write something based on the model but using different information or giving information in a different form. A typical example of this at pre-intermediate level is shown on p 74, taken from *Freewheeling 2* (Rodriguez and Barbisan 1992), a course for secondary-school students.

5 Read and complete

▶ Read the text about Teal's last day.

At nine o'clock Sir Arnold visited the dentist. Two hours later he met his old friend Eleanor Ternon at the Café Royale. At 12.30 he had lunch with Lord Parsnip, the publisher. He returned from lunch at 2.30.

Then at half past three he had to attend a meeting of the Finance Committee. It was a long meeting and he had to rush to catch his plane to Zurich. The plane left at seven fifteen.

▶◀ Now use the information to complete the police report.

POLICE REPORT

9.00 *Visited the dentist*

11.00

12.30

15.30

19.15

From *Freewheeling 2*, Rodriguez and Barbisan (Heinemann 1992)

At a more advanced level, coursebooks include more demanding tasks to link reading with writing, such as summarizing and note-taking, which require both selective processing of the written text and expressing the information selected in a different written format and style.

When analysing the **reading content** of a general coursebook, we need to consider:

- the quantity of reading material
- the type of reading passages included
- how early on reading passages are introduced in a beginners' course
- whether any help is given to learners in developing good reading strategies
- the nature and range of exercises and activities linked to the reading passages.

Concerning the texts themselves, we need to know:

- how long they are
- how authentic they are
- how complex the grammatical and discourse structure is
- what the range of vocabulary is
- whether any specialized background knowledge is needed in order to understand them.

The **types of reading material** used can vary considerably according to the coursebook writer's perception of the interests, expectations and previous experience of the learners. There are a number of dimensions here. There is **topic**: what sort of topics are included, are they interesting, challenging, topical, culturally acceptable and likely to remain fresh over the lifetime of the book? Choosing topics is not as easy as it may seem, especially when a coursebook is destined for a very wide market. Some subjects are unacceptable or taboo in certain cultures and of considerable interest and topicality in others.

Presentation of topic is also important and the use of different type-faces, simulated or real newspaper formats, colour blocks, etc can make the reading passage stand out as something special with its own identity.

We also need to look at texts from the point of view of the **authenticity** of their language, taking into account the level. We should look for a progression towards the authentic as early as possible, whilst expecting non-authentic texts to display realistic discourse structure, as discussed earlier.

The type or **genre** of text used is also important. Coursebooks use a multitude of different types, including press extracts, advertisements, instructions, recipes, information leaflets, poems, letters, transcripts of interviews, extracts from magazine stories, questionnaires, extracts from factual books such as travel guides, and extracts from novels. We should look for a range of different text types within the ability of our students, with the amount of variety increasing as learners progress through the course. Styles will of course vary with different text types and we need to be careful not to overload learners with too much stylistic variety at too early a stage.

Some coursebooks use texts which have been gapped to a greater or lesser extent, so that learners not only have to read the text with understanding, but also have to supply missing words. If this is the case, we would expect the texts to be at a lower level of difficulty in terms of language content, density of information, etc, to compensate for the added task of completing an incomplete text.

We would expect the **exercises and activities** accompanying the reading texts to help learners to read with understanding and enjoyment.

Students can be encouraged to acquire effective reading strategies such as prediction techniques, skim-reading and dealing with unfamiliar vocabulary. The activities that we might expect to find in course material include pre-reading questions or focusing activities, post-reading comprehension questions, exercises for extracting specific information from texts and pre-teaching of unfamiliar key vocabulary items.

The two examples that follow show how reading texts are handled at intermediate and upper-intermediate levels. They are from *Blueprint Intermediate* (Abbs and Freebairn 1989) and *Highlight Upper Intermediate* (Vince 1992).

THE OLYMPIC GAMES

When the next Olympic Games begin, satellites will carry T.V. pictures of the opening ceremony to millions of people thousands of miles away. From their armchairs these people will be able to see their country's athletes competing in events and maybe winning a bronze, silver or even gold medal.

When we consider the size, the spectacle and the commercialism of the modern Olympic Games, it is difficult to remember that they started in Olympia in Greece in 776 BC with only one race, a sprint, for which the prize for the winner was an olive wreath.

The idea of an international Olympic Games was conceived by a Frenchman, Baron Pierre de Coubertin and, appropriately, the first modern Olympic Games opened in Athens in 1896. Nowadays, major cities compete to host the Olympic Games, not just for the honour the Games bring, but for the vast amount of profit a host country can make.

The games have also become politically important. They can now be seen by nearly every country in the world and are therefore an ideal platform for political statements. When Soviet troops invaded Afghanistan in 1980, many countries

in the West, including Britain and the United States, boycotted the Moscow Games. In 1984 some countries decided not to send teams to the Los Angeles Games because they felt there was not enough security and that they were too commercial.

In circumstances like these, the Olympic ideal and spirit comes into question. And for athletes there is less value in winning a gold medal if the best of the world's athletes are not competing. The question is – how much longer will the Games survive if nations continue to use them as a political platform?

Before you read

1 Which country started the Olympic Games?
2 Which country was host to the last Olympic Games?
3 Name an Olympic gold medal winner in the last Olympics.
4 Apart from gold, what other medals can athletes win?
5 Why did some countries boycott the 1980 Olympics?
6 Where are the next Games going to be held?

Words to learn
compete   vast   profit
commercial   political
ideal (adj)   invade
boycott   security

1 Read the article on the left and describe:

1 the main differences between the ancient and modern Olympic Games.
2 how certain nations have used the Olympics as a political platform.

2 Read and think.

1 Why was it appropriate that the Greeks should hold the first modern Olympics?
2 How can countries make a commercial profit from holding the Games?

3 About you

1 Have you ever been to the Olympic Games or watched them on TV?
2 Which events do you prefer?
3 What other sports do you enjoy watching or taking part in?

From *Blueprint Intermediate*, Abbs and Freebairn (Longman 1989)

READING AND LISTENING 2

Pre-reading

1 How could you accidentally ruin electrical equipment such as a TV, video, toaster, or iron? What might happen?

Reading

2 Read about Martin Stephenson's accidents and decide what caused them.

ACCIDENT PRONE

Then the video and the TV set went up in smoke, and light bulbs started popping in every room of the house. Later that year Martin suspected that it was in some way his fault when a new computer went crazy in the office where he worked. 'I must have blown its mind. It made whistling noises and printed nonsense. The lights kept going out, too, and I had a lot of bad headaches.' And that summer Martin accidentally boiled his tropical fish. 'I was just wiping the outside of the tank when I touched the thermostat. It was awful, the water was steaming. I was really upset.' Now two years later he has blown up about £5,000 worth of household equip-

ment – 9 TVs, 15 toasters, three videos, 10 kettles and so many light bulbs that the electrical shop now refuses to sell him any. His wife and children have to keep

reminding him not to touch anything electrical unless he is wearing rubber gloves. He has to wear them just to switch the lights on! 'But I just keep forgetting them,' grins Martin. 'We've just had to buy a new stereo because I accidentally touched the old one The other day my electric drill burst into flames. Most electrical appliances are under guarantee, but I have ruined so many that a lot of shops have grown suspicious and I now have to go to different towns to buy replacements.' When Martin visits his bank, all the computer screens go blank. He's knocked out a pub juke-box, and can send people reeling with huge shocks.

Comprehension check

3 Are these statements about the text *true* or *false*?
   a Martin is sure that he damaged the office computer.
   b Martin put hot water into the fish tank without meaning to.
   c Martin is supposed to put on gloves before touching electrical equipment.
   d because the appliances are under guarantee the shops become suspicious.
   e People are sometimes given electric shocks by Martin.

Word search

4 Find words or phrases in the text which could be replaced by the following. They are not in the same order as the text.
   he was to blame   unhappy   caught fire
   automatic heat control   cleaning   recently
   telling him to remember   knock people backwards   bursting

Listening

5 🔊 Listen to a doctor talking about Martin's problem. Tick the points which he mentions. Explain what he says about these points.
a comb	showers
a car door	flowers
10,000 volts	weather
photographers	leather
food allergies	plants
motion of trains	
emotional strain	

6 Have you ever broken anything, or been involved in an accident of some kind? Do you think that some people are 'accident prone'?

59

From *Highlight Upper Intermediate*, Vince (Heinemann 1992)

Both these examples of reading texts have:

- pre-reading attention-focusing activities
- vocabulary learning
- comprehension checks
- extension to involve the students' personal experience.

In this way the reading text is the focus of a range of activities beginning with prediction and ending with reference to students' own experience.

At most levels, strategy-developing activities can be made explicit, encouraging learners to reflect on their learning, as in this exercise from *Cambridge Advanced English* (Jones 1991), which is based on a newspaper article that the students have already read:

B Work in pairs. Highlight these words in the article (the ¶ shows the paragraph they are in). Work out their meanings from the context. When you've decided, look them up in a dictionary to check if you were right.

articulated (¶ 1)   confused   expressed   contradicted
articulate (¶ 2)   athletic   interesting   speaking clearly   violent
oafish (¶ 2)   inaudible   noisy   idiotic
garrulous (¶ 2)   very talkative   very quiet   peace-loving   violent
preposterous (¶ 2)   enormous   muscular   ridiculous-looking
perpetrated (¶ 3)   committed   enjoyed   witnessed
inexhaustible (¶ 4)   incredible   tiring   never-ending
brief (¶ 8)   short   instructions   report   request
gleefully (¶ 8)   in dismay   joyfully   loudly   at the top of his voice

Which information in the text helped you to guess the meaning of each word?

From *Cambridge Advanced English*, Jones (CUP 1991)

Widdowson (1978) and others have shown that comprehension questions can vary in the degree of understanding of the text that is required. Some questions only require literal or surface understanding, and are usually of a straightforward factual nature. In extreme cases, comprehension questions can be answered by matching a word in the question to the same word in the text and then copying out the sentence in the text containing that word.

More demanding questions require processing of the text at a deeper level, so that information contained in different parts of the text is identified and combined to give a complete answer. Yet other questions require inference, where the reader is required to bring to bear information that is not contained in the text, but is essential for interpreting its content. Some inference questions are given in the example on p 79 from *Nexus* (Mills 1990). They are based on a long text which I have edited for the sake of brevity. The *fourth incident* referred to in the questions is the one described here.

2 The information needed to answer the following questions is in the text, but is not stated explicitly. You have to infer the answer.

a Why have Chinese restaurants always had such trouble with customers?

b In the third and fourth incidents, did the customers leave without paying?

c In the fourth incident, why was the money knocked onto the floor?

d In the fourth incident, why did the customers leave without further trouble?

What do you do when you're a Chinese waiter attacked by a customer? You don't call the police. Jacquie Hughes tells the extraordinary tale of the Diamond Four.

16   One worker from the Wong Kei told another tale. A group of customers decided to pay their bill in coins, stacking them in towers on the table. When they got up to leave, one knocked the piles over, sending the money flying. When a waiter tried to stop them leaving until it had been counted, a woman in the group hit him over the head.

The waiter—who had his hands full of dishes—pushed back. She produced police ID, and said she was going to charge him with assault. Another customer objected, and offered to be witness for the waiter. He was told to shut up, it was none of his business. When he announced he was a journalist, the group apologised and left.

Jacquie Hughes   *City Limits*

From *Nexus*, Mills (Heinemann 1990)

In his instructions for this exercise, the writer might have added that only *some* of the information needed to answer these questions is in the text. Additional information has to come from the reader's knowledge of the world; for example: what powers does a journalist have that could cause the police to apologize and leave? Here, the coursebook is quite correctly involving the learner's knowledge system and drawing on his/her knowledge of the world. This process is inherent in virtually all language use and therefore should be reflected in learning/teaching material.

Finally, we should see what is done to develop vocabulary through reading. Different types of vocabulary-teaching exercises linked to reading include the following:

- words are pre-taught because they are unfamiliar to the learners and key to understanding the text
- after reading, students undertake word-search activities, looking in the text for near-synonyms, opposites, etc of words given in the exercise
- learners use new vocabulary from the reading passage in different contexts.

▓ Checklist for reading

- ☐ Is the reading text used for introducing new language items (grammar and vocabulary), consolidating language work, etc?
- ☐ Is there a focus on the development of reading skills and strategies?
- ☐ Is the reading material linked to other skills work?
- ☐ Is there emphasis on reading for pleasure and for intellectual satisfaction?
- ☐ How many reading texts are there, and how frequently do they occur?
- ☐ How early on in the course (at elementary level) do reading texts start to appear?
- ☐ How long are the texts? Do they encourage intensive/extensive reading?
- ☐ How authentic are the texts?
- ☐ Is the subject matter appropriate (interesting, challenging, topical, varied, culturally acceptable, unlikely to date)?
- ☐ What text types *(genres)* are used? Are they appropriate?
- ☐ Are the texts complete or gapped?
- ☐ Does the material help comprehension by, for example:
  - – setting the scene
  - – providing background information
  - – giving pre-reading questions?
- ☐ What kind of comprehension questions are asked:
  - – literal (surface) questions
  - – discourse-processing questions
  - – inference questions?
- ☐ To what extent does the material involve the learner's knowledge system (knowledge of the world)?

5   Writing

Writing activities in coursebooks are normally of the controlled or guided kind, where a model is given and the student's task is to produce something similar, usually based on additional information given. The types of writing task given can be quite varied and include writing factual accounts such as a report for a newspaper, filling in grids, writing notes to others, making lists, filling in forms, writing a diary, writing formal and informal letters, summarizing texts, and many others.

As well as teaching the mechanics of writing at sentence level, we would expect writing material to familiarize learners with the way written text is organized in terms of its discourse structure. Different kinds of writing have different conventions for their organization and expression, and a coursebook should cover as many of these as is appropriate for the level and aims of the learners. At the very least, it should deal with paragraphing, which is the basic unit of organization for most kinds of written English.

The following extract from *Highlight Upper Intermediate* (Vince 1992), provides good examples of the use of controlled and guided writing exercises (Exercises 1 and 2). These lead to a much freer writing activity (Exercise 5) which is prepared by a cued discussion on eating (Exercise 3). Exercise 4 focuses on paragraphing through a re-ordering procedure which requires learners to sequence eleven sentences and put them into three paragraphs. This activity sensitizes learners to the relationship between topic development and paragraphing, each new paragraph signalling a development or a change in the topic.

WRITING

Controlled practice

1 Put each phrase into the text below.

in the middle of the morning, quite early, on weekdays, at the same time, when, every year, during the week, at weekends, then, usually, quite often, at about one o'clock, generally, occasionally, on Saturday evening

[a] _____ I don't have time for a good breakfast, and I don't [b] _____ feel like it anyway! But [c] _____ I get up [d] _____ and [e] _____ treat myself to a traditional cooked breakfast and read the paper [f] _____ . [g] _____ I do some gardening, or go shopping. [h] _____ I might have a cup of tea and a biscuit, but it depends what I'm doing. I have a light lunch [i] _____ , or very occasionally I go out to the pub for a drink and a sandwich. [j] _____ , unless we go out, I try out a new recipe from one of my large collection of cookery books. My sister gives me one [k] _____ on my birthday. But I like eating out [l] _____ and we [m] _____ go round to friends for Sunday lunch. [n] _____ I eat much less, mainly snacks [o] _____ I can find the time.

Guided writing

2 Write a description of your usual eating habits on weekdays and at weekends. Use this outline:

Most days _____
During the morning _____
At lunchtime _____
Sometimes _____
In the evening _____
At weekends _____

Pre-writing

3 Discuss eating habits in your country. Talk about these points.
popular kinds of food   national dishes   restaurants
other eating places   snacks

4 Re-organise this text so that it is in three paragraphs. The topics of the paragraphs are: food, places to eat and eating habits. The first sentence is in the correct position.

People in Britain eat many different kinds of food. [a]Most people have an evening meal at about six o'clock, but some people prefer to eat later. [b]Many people buy frozen food, and food in packets because this is more convenient. [c]Some people eat a large cooked breakfast, but this can be very fattening. [d]Food from other countries, especially Chinese and Indian food, is also popular. [e]During the day, nearly everyone drinks cups of tea or coffee. [f]Fast food and pizza restaurants are also very popular. [g]There are traditional dishes, such as roast beef, and fish and chips. [h]In most towns you can find Indian and Chinese restaurants, and sometimes more expensive French restaurants. [i]Lunch is any time between twelve and one. [j]Pubs usually serve meals, which are often more traditional food.

Writing

5 Write a description of food and eating habits in your country based on question 4.

From *Highlight Upper Intermediate*, Vince (Heinemann 1992)

The style of written English is in most cases significantly different from that of the spoken language and learners need exposure to written styles with their salient features pointed out. Writing makes use of different language resources than speech, for instance paragraphing, spelling and punctuation. We should check which of these aspects of writing are covered in the coursebook and how it is done. The example here from *Cambridge Advanced English* (Jones 1991) shows how one writer uses short extracts from texts with contrasting styles.

As well as asking learners to identify the type of text that each extract comes from, the material encourages them to think about what linguistic clues in the extracts led them to their decision. In this way students are helped to think about and talk about language and style.

In real life, writing is done with a readership in mind and writers need to know who their readers are in order to write appropriately for them. They need to judge how much knowledge of the subject their readers already have, so as not to patronize them on the one hand or mystify them on the other. Do writing activities in the coursebook take this into account?

7.4   **Different styles**   Functions

A   Work in pairs or small groups. On the next page there are ten extracts from various publications and documents. Decide together:

- What each extract is about and what topic it deals with. Try guessing from the layout and typeface before you read the extracts.
- What kind of publication or document each extract comes from.

★ Using phrases like these can help you to avoid sounding too dogmatic or even aggressive in a discussion:

> *It looks like ...... because ...*
> *It seems to me that it's ...... because ...*
> *I don't think it's ...... because ...*
> *It could either be ...... or ......*
> *It seems to be about ...... because ...*
> *I think this comes from ...... because ...*

1

This book has been specially prepared to make it enjoyable reading for people to whom English is a second or foreign language. An English writer never thinks of avoiding unusual words, so that the learner, trying to read the book in its original form, has to turn frequently to the dictionary and so loses much of the pleasure that the book ought to give.

2

Dickie Kettleson is a ten year-old boy growing up at a time when even the most ordinary life is a struggle. Dickie's world is his home and his neighbourhood – his family, his street, the threat of hunger and destruction that lurks just outside the door.

3

Most of the country will have another dry, warm day with long sunny spells, but there is the risk of one or two showers, perhaps heavy, later in the afternoon and evening.

4

Everyone must, in principle, have a visa to visit Japan. However, to help tourism, bilateral agreements with some countries mean you don't need a visa if you are from western Europe, the UK or most English-speaking countries, with the notable exceptions of the USA, Australia and South Africa.

5

Avoid listening with your headphones at a volume so loud that extended play might affect your hearing. As your headphones are of open-air design, sounds go out through the headphones. Remember not to disturb those close to you.

6

It's a dream come true when compared with making the journey by road. You don't have to contend with traffic jams, motorway hold-ups or the uncertainties of driving to the airport. You won't have to bother about parking either.

7

We found this really terrific place just a little way from the village and because the only way you could get there was on foot, it was completely unspoilt. We were practically the only people there.

8

One grey November morning I was running near the edge of a lake. On the path ahead of me an old man shuffled along slowly, using a cane. As I ran by I called out, 'Good morning!' He returned my greeting and then called after me rather unexpectedly, 'What do you gain by running?' I shouted back: 'It makes me feel good!'

9

The dose may be taken three or four times daily at intervals of not less than four hours. Do not exceed the stated dose. If symptoms persist, consult your doctor.

10

Claims under section 5 (Baggage) will not be considered unless substantiated by an original sales receipt or valuation for any item exceeding £50 or more.

B Highlight the words or information that led you to your decision about each extract. Which was the main language clue in each case?

From *Cambridge Advanced English*, Jones (CUP 1991)

Checklist for writing

☐ How does the material handle
   - controlled writing
   - guided writing
   - free or semi-free writing?
☐ Is there appropriate progression and variety of task?
☐ Are the conventions of different sorts of writing taught? If so, which ones, and how are they presented?
☐ Is paragraphing taught adequately?
☐ Is there emphasis on the style of written English? At advanced level, is there attention to different styles according to text type?
☐ Is attention given to the language resources specific to the written form, such as punctuation, spelling, layout, etc?
☐ How much emphasis is there on accuracy?
☐ Are learners encouraged to review and edit their written work?
☐ Is a readership identified for writing activities?

6   Specialized books for skills development

Several publishers have series of books at different levels, each focusing on one skill at one level. These series normally have three or four different levels and cover all four skills at each level. They generally follow the same principles that we have seen above, but contain more detailed and extensive presentation and practice material. Although the focus in each book is on one skill, other skills will also be taught in relation to the main skill area. For example, a reading skills book takes sentence linking as a focus in one unit and includes writing exercises where learners are asked to use pronouns correctly across sentence boundaries. This work on cohesion is practised through writing, but is also very important to reading, as misinterpretation of pronoun reference has been shown to be a major difficulty in interpreting text.

An advantage claimed by the skills series is flexibility in designing a package for individual students or groups who do not conform to the general coursebooks' norms for skill levels. In other words, because of previous learning experience, or for other reasons, students may not be at the same level in all four skills. The skills series allow learners to study at different levels in the different skills, something that a conventional course cannot easily accommodate.

Checklist for specialized skills books

☐ What levels are available?
☐ How do the different skills books at the same level relate to one another?
☐ Is there a communicative dimension as well as an individual skill content?
☐ How much guidance is given in working out a syllabus to meet individual student needs profiles, using skills books at different levels?

7 Readers

Readers are a valuable way of providing learners with additional exposure to the language. Very often they form the core of a class or school library which students are encouraged to use as frequently as they wish. Readers are graded according to different formulae, and students progress through the stages as their knowledge of the language and their reading skills develop.

Traditionally, readers have been graded according to vocabulary and grammatical structure. The *Longman Structural Readers* series, a long-established collection, grades in this way into six levels. Level 1 uses a basic vocabulary of 300 words and a very restricted range of structure. By level 6, which is at intermediate level, the basic vocabulary is 1800 words and the range of structures much wider.

Other series of readers have added further criteria for grading to the original ones of vocabulary and structure. The *Macmillan Bookshelf* series is divided into four levels, graded on the basis of cohesion and contextualization as well as lexis and structure. Heinemann's *New Wave Readers* series includes cohesion and reference and adds narrative expectation and information flow.

Information load is important in assessing the difficulty of reading material. Too dense an information load makes reading material difficult, no matter how controlled the structure and vocabulary. That is why simplified and abridged readers can sometimes be more difficult than the originals.

Some readers have optional cassettes containing readings of the whole text, or part of it. Some readers also have worksheets, allowing learners to assess their progress through comprehension questions, vocabulary checks, etc.

A major problem for authors of readers designed for more adult students, especially at elementary level, is making the content sophisticated enough, whilst controlling all the factors referred to above. It is important that such learners do not feel patronized through trivial or childish content. Presentation is also important in readers: a well-designed cover and professional layout can make a book more attractive and therefore more likely to be used.

Checklist for readers

☐ What is the basis of the grading? Which factors are taken into account in the series?
☐ Are accompanying cassettes available?
☐ Are there worksheets? If so, what do they contain?
☐ Is the content interesting and sophisticated enough for the readership?
☐ Is the presentation professional and attractive?

Conclusion

Skills work is an important component of any coursebook that claims to equip learners to use language in real situations. As in other aspects of materials analysis and evaluation, what you look for will depend on your needs and your learners' needs. The most important points in most circumstances are to look for a balance of skills which reflects the aims of your teaching and to check that the coursebook provides material for appropriate integrated skills work.

Chapter 7 **Topic, subject content and social values**

This chapter will deal with non-linguistic aspects of coursebooks: what topics they include, the subject matter they select and how they treat it. We will also look at the cultural settings used by coursebooks and what has sometimes been called the 'hidden curriculum': the image of life presented by coursebooks, the attitudes they convey, consciously or unconsciously, and the social and cultural values that they communicate.

1 Topic and subject content

Although language coursebooks are primarily a means for facilitating language learning, they cannot simply do that and no more, because language is used in real situations for real purposes. A study of a language solely as an abstract system would not equip learners to use it in the real world. As a consequence, coursebooks must and do represent language as it is actually used and therefore they contain subject matter and deal with topics of various kinds. Not only is this necessary, it is highly desirable from a number of viewpoints.

Learners come to class with, among other attributes, knowledge, attitudes, skills, cognitive abilities, curiosity and experience. Language learning as a process will relate to and engage these attributes so that the learning process is enriched and made more meaningful. Coursebooks can contribute to this process by including subject matter which, whilst being primarily designed for language teaching, is also informative, challenging, amusing, exciting and occasionally provocative. They can provide opportunities for expanding students' experience in general, as well as in language learning.

There is no conflict of interest here, as using English to convey information about an aspect of the real world is providing a better model of language use than describing some imaginary non-existent construct, and at the same time is more likely to motivate the learner. So this additional role of the coursebook, to include topics which will interest and inform learners, is one that we should explore. Students may learn better when they are not only concentrating on learning the target language, but are also using the language to do other things or to learn about other subjects.

At school level, we may ask ourselves whether the English coursebook limits itself to teaching language in bland contexts, or if it crosses subject boundaries (a little risky in some schools, but generally well worth the risk involved) to include material on other subjects, such as history, geography and science. At whatever level, topics which are real and immediate must command more interest and response from learners then imaginary, made-up content. For instance, the short articles from *Freewheeling 2* (Rodriguez and Barbisan 1992) about some European cities will be of interest to many learners who may already have visited one or may well hope to do so in the future.

FOCUS ON SKILLS

1.3

READING

1 Match
▶ Match the cities and the countries.

Rome	*France*
Paris	*Austria*
Vienna	*Italy*

2 Compare
▶◀ Talk to your partner about these cities. What do you know about them? What do they have in common? Make a list.

3 Check
▶◀ Now read about these cities. Can you find the things you talked about in 2?

32

Rome

Rome is the most historic of Italian cities. Known as *the eternal city* it is full of spectacular monuments from the past, such as the ancient Colosseum and the superb Trevi Fountain. Every Sunday crowds gather in St Peter's Square to see the Pope give his blessing to the people of Rome. Rome is also famous for its food: its pavement cafés are always full of visitors enjoying the pasta, pizza and Italian sunshine.

Paris

France is the largest country in Western Europe and its regions display all the variety you would expect. But Paris, its capital, is known as the most romantic city in the world. The Eiffel Tower, the River Seine, the famous Louvre Museum make it a city for lovers of art; and for fun-lovers Paris is only a few kilometres away from EuroDisney - Europe's newest theme park.

Vienna

THE NEW EUROPEAN GUIDE

Music is at the heart of Austria's capital city. Vienna, built on the banks of the beautiful Blue Danube, is the home of the waltz and even today its streets are alive with the sound of music. Visitors come from all over the world to see the horses in the famous Spanish Riding School, to hear the Vienna Boy's Choir sing in the ancient St Stephen's Cathedral or simply to sit for hours over coffee, cake and ice-cream in one of Vienna's famous cafés.

---

4 Match
▶◀ Match the pictures and the captions.

1 *The superb Trevi Fountain*
2 *The Eiffel Tower*
3 *The famous Spanish Riding School*

In which of the three cities can you find these places?

8

From *Freewheeling 2*, Rodriguez and Barbisan (Heinemann 1992)

In the text about the imaginary countries 'Fantasia' and 'Outland' in *The New Cambridge English Course 2* (Swan and Walter 1990), readers genuinely interested in the real world might be disappointed, despite the methodologically sound way in which the text is used in the book. Some may feel it to be a lost opportunity, because it would have been no more difficult for the authors to use real countries for the text, as indeed they do in a later unit when they provide a map of the western half of the United States in connection with a listening activity.

Course material which fails to include relevant and interesting topics is in danger of losing the attention of its users, and, perhaps even more seriously, is conveying an unwritten message, a sub-text. Coursebooks which contain a preponderance of vague, bland material, made up of trivial incidents which do not engage the intellect of the learner and neither inform nor challenge are in danger of saying to the learner that, despite the difficulty of language learning and the time and effort involved, there is nothing of any consequence that can be done with the language at the present stage of attainment.

The content does not necessarily have to be heavy and intellectual in order to be worthwhile: there is plenty of scope for humour and human interest stories too. We look for a degree of authenticity in materials and for a communicative approach. Really authentic material is material that creates an authentic response, that informs, challenges, stimulates, enriches experience, encourages curiosity, develops judgement, and does the other things that real language does. Interaction among learners, if it is to have a genuine value as communication, should involve the students in developing informed opinions and expressing those opinions, in forming their own conclusions and communicating those conclusions, in discussing and justifying, in influencing and being influenced by others. This can only be done if there is content at the base, and part of the role of the coursebook is to provide some of this content.

A genuinely communicative coursebook is one which not only helps to teach the mechanics of communication, but which also communicates effectively itself about worthwhile subjects and promotes meaningful communication among its users. Unless coursebooks and language teachers can achieve this, foreign language teaching will risk being a fringe subject situated on the edge of the curriculum – at the extreme, a skill-based subject without content. As Risager (1990) writes, 'One central task of future textbooks is to contribute to "cognitive mapping", ie give a structured insight into culture and society.'

14 Things have changed

Present Perfect; *used to*; *since* and *for*.

1 Complete these sentences and write them out correctly. (You may need to put more than one word in a blank.) To get the information you need, look at the statistics and the background information on Fantasia. Use a dictionary when necessary.

1. The population of Fantasia has *increased / decreased* since 1900.
2. The population of San Fantastico *increased / decreased / has increased / has decreased* since 1950.
3. Fantasia used to be highly industrialised, but now has a mainly agricultural economy. True or false?
4. The percentage of homeless people in Fantasia has *risen / fallen* considerably .... 1900.
5. Unemployment figures .... *improved / got worse* since 1950.
6. The percentage of women in paid employment has *risen / fallen* .... 1950.
7. Fantasia has just .... a .... of Friendship and Protection with Outland.
8. Outland .... to be a Fantasian Colony. It *became / has become* independent in ....
9. The Fantasians .... to have Parliamentary elections every .... years. Since 1980, they *have / had / have had* Parliamentary elections every .... years.
10. Mrs Rask *is / was / has been* President of Fantasia for .... years.
11. President Rask and Mrs Martin *know / knew / have known* each other .... a long time.
12. They *first met / have first met* at the Olympic Games in 19..............., where Mrs Rask *won / has won* a silver medal for the high jump.

FANTASIA AND OUTLAND: SOME BACKGROUND INFORMATION

Since the revolution in 1886, Fantasia has been a parliamentary democracy. There are two Houses of Parliament: elections to both used to be held every seven years, but since the Electoral Reform Act of 1980, elections have been held every four years. The President is elected separately by popular vote; the last presidential election was held three years ago. Mrs Kirsten Rask, the current President, is a distinguished physicist. She is also a former Olympic athlete who won a silver medal for the high jump in the 1960 Games.

Outland was formerly the Fantasian colony of South Wesk, but has been independent since the end of the War of Independence in 1954. Relations between the two countries have become more friendly since Mrs Rask's election, and Fantasia has just signed a 'Treaty of Friendship and Protection' with Outland. President Martin of Outland was at University with the Fantasian President's husband, Dr Erasmus Rask, and Mrs Martin and President Rask have been friends since they met at the 1960 Olympics.

STATISTICS	1900	1950	TODAY
Population	20m	35m	46m
Population of San Fantastico	1m	4m	3m
Average number of children per family	4.5	3.6	2
Working week (hours)	54	49	42
Paid holiday (weeks per year)	0	2	5
Size of army	500,000	200,000	50,000
Homeless	23%	17%	8%
Unemployment	20%	7%	17%
Women in paid employment	18%	23%	79%
Percentage of workforce in agriculture	84%	66%	19%
Contribution of agriculture to Gross National Product	78%	51%	8%
Contribution of industry to Gross National Product	11%	38%	83%
Foreign tourists per year	?	30,000	6m

2 How have you changed since you were a small child? How has your village/town/country changed? Useful structures:

I used to . . . , but now I . . .
People used to . . . , but now they . . .

From *The New Cambridge English Course 2*, Swan and Walter (CUP 1990)

▨ Checklist for topic and subject content

☐ Are real topics included in the coursebook? If so, how varied are they?
☐ Will the coursebook contribute to expanding learners' awareness and enriching their experience?
☐ Does it relate to and engage the learners' knowledge system, ie the knowledge of the world that they bring with them?
☐ Are the topics sophisticated enough in content for the learners, but at the right level linguistically?
☐ Do they actually do what they set out to do? If informative, do they inform, if humorous, do they amuse, if controversial, do they challenge, etc?
☐ Are they suitable for the age group?
☐ At school level, do they link in with other subjects (eg history, geography, science)?

2 Social and cultural values

On a more practical plane, we need to ensure that the coursebook sets its material in social and cultural contexts that are comprehensible and recognizable to the learners, in terms of location, social mores, age group, etc. In addition to the physical context, the relationships, modes of behaviour and intentions of the characters in the book should be interpretable by the students, so that they can relate the language used to its purpose in the social context.

If they have any subject content, coursebooks will directly or indirectly communicate sets of social and cultural values which are inherent in their make-up. This is the so-called 'hidden curriculum' which forms part of any educational programme, but is unstated and undisclosed. It may well be an expression of attitudes and values that are not consciously held but which nevertheless influence the content and image of the teaching material, and indeed the whole curriculum.

A curriculum (and teaching materials form part of this) cannot be neutral because it has to reflect a view of social order and express a value system, implicitly or explicitly. It has been claimed by some educationalists that this hidden curriculum is more effective than the stated official curriculum because it pervades most aspects of education. Risager (1990) suggests that

> foreign language teaching textbooks no longer just develop concurrently with the development of foreign language pedagogy in a narrow sense, but they increasingly participate in the general cultural transmission within the educational system and in the rest of society.

Because the underlying value system is not explicit and is unstated, it is necessary to look at coursebooks in some detail in order to unearth what some of their unstated values are. This is a different perspective from that of language content or methodology but it is at least as important, because the value system of a coursebook can influence the perceptions and attitudes of learners generally and towards learning English in particular.

The representation of men and women in language teaching materials is the subject of some research (Jenkins, cited in Littlejohn and Windeatt 1989) showing a direct correlation between the length of time spent using the *Alpha One Reading Program* (which was said to portray girls as stupid, dependent, whining and fearful, and boys as active and aggressive) and the degree to which pupils' attitudes matched those in the materials.

Sexism and gender are not the only concerns in this domain, but they have become among the most actively pursued and in some quarters politicized. It is of considerable interest to explore how coursebooks portray women in relation to men, and whether they project a positive image with which female students can identify.

One of the main aims of such an analysis is to identify unrepresentative negative stereotypes, such as women regularly being shown as housewives or being seen as only able to attain fulfilment in life through their man or being portrayed as illogical and excessively emotional. Where such stereotypes are unearthed, they can be taken into account in evaluating material for future use, or, if the material is already in use, they can be identified, confronted and discussed openly with students. This sort of stereotyping can occur occasionally in a coursebook or it can be pervasive. The occasional occurrence can be confronted and discussed, and may in fact provide useful teaching material, although unintended by the writers. Pervasive negative stereotyping is more serious and if it offends sensibilities it may well cause the coursebook not to be used.

Gender differences are not the only area of possible discrimination or unflattering portrayal. It is also illuminating to look at materials to see if and how they represent people according to the following categories:

- ethnic origin
- occupation
- age
- social class
- disability.

The same kinds of questions can be asked about them as about the portrayal of women.

Another area of interest is the nature of the characters depicted in the coursebook. What do we learn about what makes them tick, what motivates them, about their fears, hopes, loves and hates? The affective aspect of characters, their feelings and subjectivity are seriously under-represented in many coursebooks, making them less than complete people.

A final perspective on the value systems embodied in coursebooks is that of society and social structures. In some coursebooks the characters exist in some kind of social network, whether the focus is on the family, the peer group or the workplace, and interact with one another. But in others, characters pop up from nowhere, sometimes just as disembodied voices in a dialogue, and disappear just as quickly. This fragmented portrayal of social relationships (or lack of them) does little to give credibility to the characters, does not help learners to relate to them and provides little context for meaningful language learning.

▣ Checklist for social and cultural values

- ☐ Are the social and cultural contexts in the coursebook comprehensible to the learners?
- ☐ Can learners interpret the relationships, behaviour, intentions, etc of the characters portrayed in the book?
- ☐ Are women given equal prominence to men in all aspects of the coursebook?
- ☐ What physical and character attributes are women given?
- ☐ What professional and social positions are women shown as occupying?
- ☐ What do we learn about the inner lives of the characters?
- ☐ To what extent is the language of feeling depicted?
- ☐ Do the coursebook characters exist in some kind of social setting, within a social network?
- ☐ Are social relationships portrayed realistically?

3   Case study: subject content and values in coursebooks

I took a representative sample of six general coursebooks at elementary and pre-intermediate levels, all published between 1986 and 1992, and looked at them using the checklist below. Three of the courses were for adults and the other three were for secondary-school students.

- range of topic
- inclusion of sensitive social/cultural topics
- characters depicted:
  - representation of women
  - portrayal of gender role
  - age
  - social class
  - ethnic origin
  - occupation/profession
  - disability
- social relationships
  - family make-up
  - social networks
- expression of personal feelings
- interactions
  - transactions (functional interactions)
  - personal interactions

The range of topics varies considerably. In the books for secondary schools, there are between eight and fifteen different topics dealt with in one book. The scope and depth of treatment also vary from very patchy to reasonably substantial, taking the language level into account. Common topics include travel and tourism, wildlife, famous people (past and present) and teenage lifestyles. Examples of less common topics are design and ballooning. All the topics seem likely to appeal to at least a fair proportion of teenagers and the presentation in two of the books is of a high standard, with texts presented realistically and accompanied by good-quality visuals.

Some topics are included which cross traditional subject boundaries; for instance one book has texts on aspects of geography and history. But the boundary crossing is limited and not sustained. Most of the topics deal with different aspects of everyday life which would be of interest to teenagers.

The three books for adults differ more significantly in the range of topics covered, from nine to twenty. Again there are significant differences in the scope and depth of treatment of the topics. Some are transparent pretexts for language work but others are well presented and developed. The only common topic is travel and tourism, seemingly a perennial in EFL materials, but crime and police work are also well represented. Leisure activities and work are also well in evidence. One of the three courses includes the environment, and the same course has an innovative unit on moral issues.

Sensitive socio-cultural topics are dealt with in two of the six books (one for schools and one for adults). The topics covered include people in need, homelessness, physical handicap, world poverty and discrimination. These topics are not dealt with extensively, but they are given sufficient prominence not to be the product of tokenism.

Turning now to the characters depicted in the coursebooks, it was reassuring to see that women and girls, in number, are represented equally with men and boys. In terms of gender role, the picture is more mixed. One book seemed to me to be male focused, depicting men in action roles, in control of the situation, and women in subordinate roles, the secretary being told what to do by her boss, the housewife being duped by a con-man, and the girl being rescued by a helicopter winch man. However, it should be added in fairness that another unit, again male focused, humorously portrays the husband as a secret busker whilst his wife is a dentist.

Interestingly, on the subject of people saving each other, it is nearly always the male who does the saving and the female who is saved – another aspect of the active male image contrasted with the passive female image. This may or may not be acceptable, depending entirely on the value system of the users of the material. I do not feel that there are necessarily any moral universals here (so long as we avoid an aggressor–victim scenario), and local cultural norms have to be taken into account and respected.

Three out of the six books have topics on famous people. In one, eight out of nine are men, in another, four out of five are men, and in the third, six out of six are men. Eighteen out of twenty is unbalanced, even if there are more famous men than women in history!

In contrast, one book, *Flying Colours 2* (see p 94), has a section on women of achievement and in a separate section focuses on the role of women in society and in employment in particular.

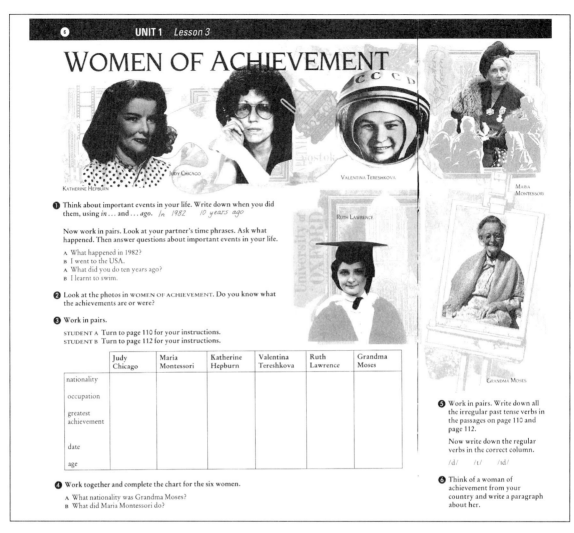

6   **UNIT 1** *Lesson 3*

WOMEN OF ACHIEVEMENT

KATHERINE HEPBURN

JUDY CHICAGO

VALENTINA TERESHKOVA

MARIA MONTESSORI

RUTH LAWRENCE

GRANDMA MOSES

1 Think about important events in your life. Write down when you did them, using *in* ... and ... *ago*. *In 1982   10 years ago*

Now work in pairs. Look at your partner's time phrases. Ask what happened. Then answer questions about important events in your life.

A What happened in 1982?
B I went to the USA.
A What did you do ten years ago?
B I learnt to swim.

2 Look at the photos in WOMEN OF ACHIEVEMENT. Do you know what the achievements are or were?

3 Work in pairs.

STUDENT A Turn to page 110 for your instructions.
STUDENT B Turn to page 112 for your instructions.

	Judy Chicago	Maria Montessori	Katherine Hepburn	Valentina Tereshkova	Ruth Lawrence	Grandma Moses
nationality						
occupation						
greatest achievement						
date						
age						

4 Work together and complete the chart for the six women.

A What nationality was Grandma Moses?
B What did Maria Montessori do?

5 Work in pairs. Write down all the irregular past tense verbs in the passages on page 110 and page 112.

Now write down the regular verbs in the correct column.

/d/   /t/   /ɪd/

6 Think of a woman of achievement from your country and write a paragraph about her.

From *Flying Colours 2*, Garton-Sprenger and Greenall (Heinemann 1991)

In terms of age, the majority of the characters represent the ages of the learners for whom the books are destined. So, for the school books, most characters are youngish teenagers. Adults, where they appear, tend to be shadowy creatures who exist solely in their role as parent, youth group organizer, police officer, teacher, etc. This is probably a very good reflection of the teenager's view of the world!

Adult courses show people in their twenties going about their everyday lives and occasionally doing something more adventurous. Additionally, there is the occasional elderly professor, pensioner or castle proprietor, but the world of the adult coursebook is seriously centred on the early to mid-twenties.

Social class is barely evident and we might think that a classless society had finally really arrived, at least in the world of the coursebook. Closer analysis shows that this world is definitely middle class, again reflecting the users of the books. In one exercise on occupations, all eight professions listed are middle class, although in other exercises the occasional waiter, cleaner, etc is included.

In all the books people of different ethnic origins (ie not white British or American) appear, although in some cases they are simply represented in the visuals and do not have much of a role in the presentations or story line. Where they do have an on-going presence it is usually in a supporting role. In most cases the representation of people of different ethnic origins appears to go beyond tokenism, but falls short of full involvement. However, in one case where the setting is an international summer camp for teenagers, there is rather more varied ethnic and national representation, as can be seen from the example below.

From *Freewheeling 2*, Rodriguez and Barbisan (Heinemann 1992)

Disability gets very little place at all, but I did locate a picture of one person in a wheelchair in *The New Cambridge English Course 2* (Swan and Walter 1990).

It is interesting to note that ethnic minority characters and people with disabilities figure more centrally in American coursebooks. This is probably because issues of ethnicity and disability have a higher profile in the United States and coursebooks would be criticized if they did not reflect this awareness.

The portrayal of social relationships in the six coursebooks differs considerably. Only two of the books have characters who continue to appear throughout as part of a developing storyline, and who could therefore be shown to have a network of changing social relationships. In one case the context is a summer camp and in the other a family which is visited by an American relative. There is some character development in one case, including a little romantic interest, but otherwise characters are portrayed fairly impersonally, as they conduct the various functional transactions of their lives.

Only one book presents any real image of family life, so there was no real opportunity to analyse which sorts of families are portrayed in coursebooks. The answer in most cases seems to be none. In some of the books examined, characters simply appear from nowhere to participate in a dialogue or exercise, without any real identity, only to disappear again for ever once the activity is over. It makes one think metaphorically of EFL puppeteers pulling their puppets out of a bag when they are needed and stuffing them away again when they have played their part.

Expressions of personal feelings are also almost completely absent, with just the occasional reference in a few of the books. The one exception is the book intended for teenagers which has a little romantic interest and which, in the context of its developing plot, includes some element of feeling and the language to express it. It will come as no surprise to note finally that the interactions which occur in great number in all the books are overwhelmingly of an impersonal, transactional nature.

There are arguments for and against having a developing storyline in a coursebook, depending on the type of teaching programme being offered, the continuity or otherwise of the students' attendance and the interests and expectations of the learners. However, unless there is a strong cultural or organizational reason to the contrary, on balance we might look to material writers to give us full, rounded characters, with whom we can identify and empathize, living in a recognizable social context.

Chapter 8 Methodology

One of the functions of coursebooks is to present the language in such a way that it is learned as effectively and quickly as possible. This implies that the coursebook writers have a view on how language is learned and how it is best taught. Although the coursebook may not seek to impose a rigid methodology on learners and teachers, nevertheless the way it organizes its material and the kind of activities it promotes can have a profound influence on what happens in the classroom. The purpose of this chapter is to explore how coursebooks see the learning process, how they view the needs and roles of learners and how they can help learners to learn.

1 Learner needs

It is surprising how few courses discuss student needs in the introductory sections of their teachers' books and even more surprising to see how many launch straight away into a description of the course and how to use it without considering, however briefly, the needs of the students for whom the course has been written. Among the exceptions to this generalization is *Blueprint One* (Abbs and Freebairn 1990), which, perhaps optimistically in the light of events since 1990, states that 'students in the 1990s live in a world where political, economic and cultural barriers are rapidly disappearing'. The authors identify five needs experienced by beginner students when learning a language in a classroom with a teacher and a textbook. These are:

- the need to communicate effectively
- the need to be familiar with the language systems
- the need for challenge
- the need to take on more responsibility for their own learning
- the need for cross-cultural awareness.

The authors of *The New Cambridge English Course* (Swan and Walter 1990) identify the need to respect the learner, adding that 'people generally learn languages best when their experience, knowledge of the world, interests and feelings are involved, and a course must allow students to be themselves as fully as possible.'

However, most courses do not discuss student needs explicitly, although their approach to their students will be implicit in the methodology they use.

Checklist for learner needs

- ☐ Does the material discuss and identify areas of student need?
- ☐ If this is not done explicitly, can the approach be inferred from the teacher's book or from the material itself?
- ☐ Is the book sensitive to what students need in order to learn well?
- ☐ If so, is this awareness reflected in the content and approach of the coursebook?

2   Guiding principles

It is illuminating to consider the general principles that underlie the actual methodological procedures adopted by courses, and these principles are made explicit in the case of several courses. Here we will examine some of them and see if there are common themes which will justify the methodology used. *Formula One* (White and Williams 1989) identifies these five principles:

- exposure to systematically controlled language helps learners
- teaching is more effective when the teacher has a clearly defined set of procedures
- learning is helped by having interesting content and situations
- learning the grammatical system is helped by having students think about rules for themselves
- personalization of content helps to ensure involvement by the learners.

In *The New Cambridge English Course* (Swan and Walter 1990) the principles of methodology are as follows:

- communicative practice resembling real-life communication
- creative use of language
- positive attitude towards error
- balance of regularity and variety in the material
- necessity of study and memorization
- learning and acquisition both catered for through intensive study of language items and tasks involving 'untidy' texts with only partial understanding
- use of the mother tongue and bilingual dictionaries where appropriate.

For *Connect* (Revell 1990) the basic principles are these:

- accuracy and fluency are both important
- structures and functions should both be taught
- grammar rules should be made explicit at some stage
- vocabulary is of prime importance
- language and tasks should be personalized wherever possible
- students should learn other things as they learn English
- a coursebook should provide interesting content
- a coursebook should also be interesting in the way that it presents its content
- all four skills should be practised in an integrated way and separately
- the students should do and say as much as possible
- a coursebook should be as comprehensive as possible.

As a final example, *Grapevine* (Viney, P. and K. 1990) proposes these 'first principles':

- a co-operative, non-judgmental atmosphere in the classroom
- an emphasis on communicative goals
- transparent teaching points (ie teachers need not teach rules explicitly)
- a clear carefully-ordered syllabus
- vocabulary development strategies
- a balanced approach to skills development

- variety of classroom activity
- varied and interesting contexts
- recognition of the broader educational context.

These principles cover a broad range and some, such as those concerning the syllabus or the subject content, are not directly concerned with methodology in its more specific sense. However others directly address how we teach the language: which general approach and specific techniques we adopt.

The main themes of the principles identified above, where they refer to methodology, are these:

- there should be controlled presentation of language
- rules need to be learned, either inductively or deductively
- there should be a balance of accuracy and fluency
- skills need to be learned both separately and in an integrated way
- communicative practice should resemble real-life language use
- learning and acquisition each have their place
- learners should be actively and fully involved in lessons
- learners should use language creatively, and activities should be personalized where possible
- learning activities should be varied
- learning should take place in a non-judgemental atmosphere and there should be a positive attitude to error
- use of the mother tongue and bilingual dictionaries is justified where it supports learning.

Most of the above is self-explanatory and can form the basis for evaluation criteria, but a few points may need discussion. The references to **learning** and **acquisition** here distinguish between intensive study of carefully controlled language input on the one hand, and a less detailed study of 'rough-tuned' language on the other hand.

The terms **inductive** and **deductive** learning need defining here as they are sometimes used in different ways. **Inductive learning** refers to the sort of learning where the starting point consists of examples of language which illustrate a rule, without the rule being stated. From the carefully chosen examples, learners are able to hypothesize about what the rule might be and then check their hypothesis, either against further examples or by creating instances of language themselves and getting feedback from the teacher as to whether they are correct or not. This is thought to resemble the way in which children acquire their mother tongue and is therefore considered by some language teachers to be more natural than deductive learning.

Deductive learning refers to the sort of learning process where explicit rules are given and learners seek to understand these rules and then produce correct sentences, etc based on them, perhaps with the help of a few examples given in the book. Rules are given to learners, without having to be worked out, and this may seem to be an easier way of learning. However, the rules are often complex and abstract, requiring a lot of understanding. Furthermore, it can be more difficult to understand and use a rule if it has not been seen embodied in a substantial number of examples.

There is no right or wrong approach here. Students learn differently, and in any case the two processes can be used to support each other. Many coursebooks introduce new items inductively and then consolidate learners' understanding by giving the rules explicitly, often in a 'language study section' at the end of each unit. This is a safe procedure because students who learn better by one process or the other are all catered for.

On balance, coursebook writers seem to prefer an inductive approach, but recognize that an element of rule-giving is sometimes necessary. *Flying Colours 2* Teacher's Book (Garton-Sprenger and Greenall 1991) illustrates this view well:

> Inductive grammar
> In keeping with the spirit of developing learner training strategies, much of the grammar is presented in an inductive way, where examples of a given target structure are presented and learners are then encouraged to work out the grammatical rules for themselves. If they wish to confirm or consolidate their conclusions, the relevant *Structures to Learn* section provides a more explicit grammatical explanation.

Inductive learning is actively promoted in an innovative way in *The New Cambridge English Course 3* (Swan and Walter 1990), where, as in the example below, learners are given examples of a particular structure and asked to decide which of several different rules is correct.

GRAMMAR: INFINITIVES AND *-ING* FORMS

2 Some of the sentences in the box have infinitives and the others have *-ing* forms. Look at the rules, and decide which one gives the best explanation.

> I would love **to learn** judo.
> We expect **to win** the basketball championship.
> If you want **to camp** here, you have to register at the office.
> I like **dancing**.
> When did you start **playing** the piano?
> I'm going to stop **boxing** – I'm getting too old.

Rules
1. We use infinitives to say what people do, and *-ing* forms to say what happens to people.
2. We use *-ing* forms to talk about the present and past, and infinitives to talk about the future.
3. We use *-ing* forms after most verbs.
4. We use infinitives after most verbs.
5. We use infinitives after some verbs and *-ing* forms after others.

From *The New Cambridge English Course 3*, Swan and Walter (CUP 1990)

The correct rule is given in the grammar summary at the end of the unit, and only one of the five choices is right. Being presented with four incorrect rules may however disconcert some teachers and students, particularly those who are used to education systems whose aims are largely based on the direct transmission of knowledge from teacher to student.

Most current materials are process-oriented in that they assume that teaching is a matter of negotiation with learners and has a concern for communication. Knowledge, in this context, is seen not as a static external entity 'out there' which has to be transmitted, but as a dynamic, changing entity, which learners can approach through experience and discovery, sometimes finding their own route.

Whatever the approach, virtually all modern language-teaching materials take a cognitive view of the learning process (whether inductive or deductive learning is favoured), in that learners are seen as conscious, thinking people with individuality and intelligence. A few remnants of behaviourist-inspired teaching techniques may survive in the use of choral repetition or mechanical drilling, and they may well have a place in certain circumstances, but the cognitive approach generally adopted is exemplified by the use of problem-solving activities, rule giving and concept checking.

Checklist for principles and approaches

- ☐ Does the coursebook make its guiding principles clear?
- ☐ Does it encourage an inductive or deductive approach to learning – or a balance of both?
- ☐ Does it have a view on accuracy and fluency?
- ☐ How does it approach the teaching of skills and communication?
- ☐ Are learners encouraged to use language creatively?
- ☐ Are any learning activities personalized?
- ☐ Is any distinction made between learning and acquisition?
- ☐ What is the attitude towards learner error?
- ☐ What is the attitude towards the use of students' mother tongue?
- ☐ Is the coursebook essentially process-oriented or product-oriented?

3   Procedures for learning and teaching

Learning a new item is facilitated if the learner can relate it, through similarity, comparison or contrast, with something that is already known and familiar. The learning process is essentially bound up with extending knowledge, understanding and skills from the familiar to the unfamiliar. In the foreign language learning situation, such a relationship could be established with the learners' native language (L1) or with what is already known of the target language (L2) or it could be established with something non-linguistic such as a picture, an action, an object or a sound. Course materials may use any or all of these procedures to structure and contextualize the learning process.

It is important that new items are controlled in terms of quantity and difficulty. Also, as we have seen earlier, if an inductive approach is taken, the examples of language given and practised must be representative of the rule that is being taught. An obvious example of this is that, where a new verb form or tense is being taught for regular verbs, irregular verbs should be kept out.

Language is a highly structured, interrelated system and consequently it is imperative that language items should be learned in relation to one another. This applies equally to grammar and lexis. Presented in a relationship of comparison, language items tend to define one another in terms of what they mean and what they do not mean. It is just as important to know what a structure or word doesn't mean as to know what it does mean. It is not possible to know the full range of meaning of a language item without also knowing the limits of that range of meaning.

Practice material is controlled to a greater or lesser extent, and coursebooks should ideally offer a variety of activities with different degrees of control, so that learners and teachers can select those which are most appropriate to their needs.

For **vocabulary**, we can apply the same principles of presenting the items in context and in a clear relationship with one another. Lists of unrelated words are difficult to learn because the words appear in isolation and, lacking any context, do not appear to the learner to have any real meaning. Presenting new lexis in association with visuals, or in a text, has the built-in advantage that the words are encountered in a context, whether non-linguistic (visual) or linguistic (text). Context makes the meaning clearer and allows students to work out the meanings of unfamiliar words using contextual and other clues, thus encouraging good communicative strategies. Therefore in our course material we should look for the presentation of vocabulary in a meaningful context. Vocabulary expansion activities can similarly exploit relationships that exist within the lexicon of English, such as synonyms or near-synonyms, opposites and hyponyms. Recycling of new vocabulary in different contexts is also necessary to ensure effective learning, so we should explore how systematically the coursebook recycles new items.

The amount of new lexis to be taught in any one unit is a debatable point, but in normal circumstances the number of new words in a text should not exceed five per cent of the total. This is to ensure a reasonable learning load and also to ensure that there are sufficient familiar words in the text to provide a comprehensible context for attempting to work out the meanings of the new words.

The use of **visuals** for presentation and practice in order to provide meaningful contexts is almost universal in coursebooks and forms one of the planks of language-teaching methodology. Whether the visuals are in colour or not, whether they are photographs or line drawings or even rather ugly cartoons affects the appearance of the material, but evaluating them from that perspective is really a matter of personal taste. However, when looking at coursebooks it is important to consider whether the visuals are an integral part of the teaching material or are there simply for decorative purposes, to make the page look better. Whilst attractively presented materials are desirable, visuals which have a teaching purpose are clearly more central to the coursebook. (Of course visuals can serve both purposes at the same time, and this would be a positive feature.)

In the two examples on pp 104–5 taken from *The Beginners' Choice* (Mohamed and Acklam 1992), whilst both are clearly relevant to the two topics being covered, the striking picture of the clocks is integral to the coursebook material because it is an essential part of Exercise 2. The picture of the Virgin Megastore, whilst relevant to the listening activity, is not an integral part of it and is therefore less central as teaching material.

Checklist for learning/teaching procedures

- ☐ How are new grammar items presented and practised?
- ☐ To what extent is the presentation and practice:
  - – related to what learners already know and to what has already been taught
  - – appropriately controlled and organized
  - – representative of the grammar rule to be learned
  - – relevant to learners' needs and interests?
- ☐ How is new vocabulary presented (eg in wordlists, in a text, with visuals)?
- ☐ How is the meaning of new vocabulary taught?
- ☐ Is there vocabulary development material, eg based on semantic relations or relations of form?
- ☐ Is new vocabulary recycled adequately?
- ☐ How much new vocabulary is presented in each unit, text, etc?
- ☐ Are visuals used extensively in the material?
- ☐ Are they reasonably well produced and attractive?
- ☐ Is the style of the visuals (eg photographs, line drawings, cartoons) acceptable to the users?
- ☐ Are visuals used as an integral part of teaching material or are they essentially decorative?

2 Opening time

About + numbers 10-12, 15, 30, 45;
What time is it?; am/pm

2 Vocabulary: the time

1 Revision

1 Make a list.

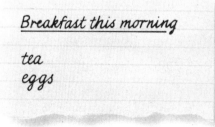

Breakfast this morning

tea

eggs

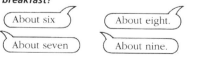

2 Answer this question – *What time do you have breakfast?*

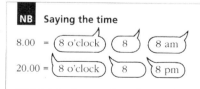

About six

About seven

About eight.

About nine.

2 Vocabulary: the time

1 Match the times to the clocks.

seven o'clock	five o'clock	eight fifteen
nine thirty	six forty-five	ten forty-five
eleven thirty	twelve fifteen	

2 Work with another student. Point at the clocks on this page. Ask and answer, like this:

What time is it?   Seven o'clock.

3 Tell another student. What time is it now?

NB Saying the time

8.00 = (8 o'clock) (8) (8 am)

20.00 = (8 o'clock) (8) (8 pm)

Which is in the morning – 8 am or 8 pm?
Which is in the evening – 8 am or 8 pm?

---

8 Listening

1 🖳 Listen to an interview about Richard Branson, the British businessman. Complete these sentences.

He finished school in . . .
He started work in . . .
He opened his first shop in . . .
He made his first £1,000,000 in . . .

2 Listen again. What questions did the interviewer ask?

3 🖳 Listen to the pronunciation of these three regular verbs. Do they end with /d/, /t/ or /ɪd/?

finished
started
opened

From *The Beginners' Choice*, Mohamed and Acklam (Longman 1992)

4 The student's role

Relatively few coursebooks have anything very explicit to say about the learner's role in the language-learning process, but it is clear from the nature of the material that students are expected to hypothesize about rules, participate actively in learning activities, relate material to their own experiences and personal lives and undertake a variety of tasks which involve problem solving of one sort or another.

A coursebook which does devote some space in its teacher's book to discussion of the role of the students is *New Dimensions* (Lonergan and Gordon 1986) which says:

> Throughout the course, students are encouraged to contribute their experience of their first language and any knowledge of English they may already have.
> A typical learning sequence might be as follows:
> Before a lesson on a new language area, students turn to the workbook and cassette for simple self-preparation exercises. Students have to muster their own learning devices and skills to enter this new language area: they listen to the new spoken language as often as they wish; they see some of the key phrases or sentences in their workbook; they will probably use a dictionary to find out meanings of key words. The learners thus enter class already partly equipped, by means of their own skills, to tackle the new area of language.

Coursebooks often show awareness that students have different learning styles and that these should be respected as far as possible. *Highlight Upper Intermediate* (Vince 1992), for example, advises teachers to 'bear in mind that learning style varies greatly from individual to individual.' The authors of *The New Cambridge English Course* (Swan and Walter 1990) say that 'students have their own ideas about language learning. Up to a point these must be respected – individuals have different learning strategies, and will not respond to methods which they distrust.' The qualification here is followed up by advice to the teacher of a rather more prescriptive nature: 'However, learners sometimes resist important and useful activities which do not fit in with their preconceptions, and this can hinder progress. So you may have to spend time training students in new attitudes to language learning.' Changing people's attitudes is notoriously difficult, and conscious attempts to do so often fail, however well intentioned. Teachers have to find a balance between respecting individual students' learning styles and trying to persuade them that, in some cases, it might be more effective to adopt different styles.

As learners progress in the language, the way they learn should progress too, as they become more familiar with the methodology and more confident in their success. An increased degree of learner autonomy, the ability to learn independently, and even to set one's own learning objectives and monitor them, should be encouraged by coursebooks through the provision of material suitable for individual study. This will usually take the form of a workbook, or it may be additional reading material or self-study cassettes. With this individual study material we would expect to see guidance on how to use it, cross-referencing from the main course to the workbook, etc, and a key to exercises, so that students can monitor their own progress.

Checklist for the student's role

- ☐ Does the material expect an active input from learners?
- ☐ Is the coursebook sensitive to different learning styles and can it accommodate them?
- ☐ Does the material provide additional material for independent study based on material already taught, eg a workbook, students' cassettes for home study, additional reading material?
- ☐ If so, is guidance provided on how to proceed?
- ☐ Is there a key for self-monitoring?

5   Study skills

Including advice and guidance for students on learning techniques within a general coursebook is a relatively recent phenomenon, but several current courses now offer study skills support to their users, usually on a regular basis throughout the course. The sections devoted to study skills focus mainly on three different aspects:

- inviting learners to reflect on how they learn, and on which ways of learning seem to be most effective for them
- offering advice to learners on ways of developing their study skills
- training learners in reference skills for using dictionaries and grammar books.

These examples illustrate how learners are provided with study skills material of different kinds:

TALK ABOUT LEARNING

Give your opinion
▶ Look at your results of the Progress Check for Units 1-5. Choose two things you got right in WORDS and GRAMMAR. Why do you think you remembered some things better than others?
▶◀ Compare what you remembered and the reasons. Did you get the same things right as your partner? Did you make the same mistakes?
■ What are the most common strategies for remembering things? Make a list.

TALK ABOUT LEARNING

Give your opinion
▶ Your teacher will give you the title of a story. Write the first paragraph on your own.
▶◀ Write the first paragraph again together. Compare with the one you wrote before. Which is better? Why?
■ Did writing with a classmate help you create a better text?

From *Freewheeling 2*, Rodriguez and Barbisan (Heinemann 1992)

LEARNING TO LEARN

Would the following three suggestions help you to learn? Discuss with the other students.

1 Set yourself realistic targets and a time limit to reach them, e.g. using a new language point in some practical way, preferably outside the classroom, by the end of the week.
2 At the end of the day read through what you have done in class, and every so often review the work you did in previous classes.
3 Keep a language learning diary and note down:

- language-learning activities you have done, e.g. "listened to the radio, understood main points" or "eavesdropped on a conversation in a cafe, able to understand most of it and realized they were cross with each other"
- problem areas you have encountered, e.g. "giving up reading the newspaper, even with the help of a dictionary it was too difficult"

From *Fast Forward 2*, Black *et al* (OUP 1987)

⑩ Find out more about your dictionary. Does it have these features?

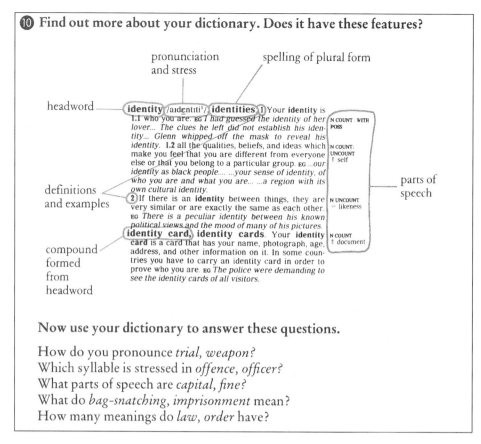

Now use your dictionary to answer these questions.

How do you pronounce *trial, weapon?*
Which syllable is stressed in *offence, officer?*
What parts of speech are *capital, fine?*
What do *bag-snatching, imprisonment* mean?
How many meanings do *law, order* have?

From *Flying Colours 2*, Garton-Sprenger and Greenall (Heinemann 1991)

In connection with guidance on study skills, students are encouraged to take some degree of responsibility for their own learning, a concept which goes hand-in-hand with moves for greater learner autonomy.

Checklist for study skills

☐ Are study skills sections included in the material?
☐ If so, do they cover these aspects:
　– reflection on study techniques
　– advice on study skills development
　– reference skills
　– other?
☐ Are students encouraged to take some degree of responsibility for their learning?

Chapter 9 Teachers' books

1   The teacher's role

How do coursebooks view the role of the teacher? Several books discuss this in their teachers' books in varying degrees of detail. *Grapevine* (Viney, P. and K. 1990) emphasizes that there is no one correct way of teaching and adds that there isn't a *Grapevine* style of teaching, despite the very detailed guidance given in the teacher's book. Just as students have different learning styles which should be respected, so teachers have different teaching styles, often partly the product of their personalities, which will mean that the same material can be taught in quite different styles.

> One teacher may be extrovert and amusing, another may be quiet and sympathetic, a third may be highly organised and disciplined [...] Books can give plans, but they can never show you how to relate to a number of individuals in a particular place on a particular day.
> (*Grapevine* Teacher's Book 1)

What this emphasizes is a fundamental principle that we have already seen earlier: the coursebook is there to aid students and teachers in numerous ways but it is not there to dictate a rigid predetermined method by which the language shall be taught and learned.

Learning and teaching are not wholly predictable activities, and even teachers who know their classes well often have to make adjustments to their planned lessons to accommodate an unexpected difficulty encountered in an item to be taught, or to respond to the mood of a class on a particular day. How much less can coursebook writers, expert in their own field but knowing little or nothing of your particular class and your style of teaching, provide foolproof material that requires no adaptation or selective use. Of course coursebook writers realize this and recommend that teachers should feel free to make changes where they feel it to be necessary and in the students' interest.

So it is ultimately the teacher, informed by feedback from students, who makes decisions, aided when appropriate by the teacher's book. These decisions may be macro decisions, such as deciding which course to use or planning a year's work, or they might be micro decisions which are taken quickly as a lesson progresses, such as deciding to do an extra exercise on a grammar topic or postponing a listening activity until a later lesson.

At all points, from selecting a whole course to omitting certain exercises to adapting a communicative activity, the prerogative lies with the teacher, who should not hesitate to make the necessary decisions if they seem appropriate. It is interesting to note that some courses offer advice on making changes at micro level to meet differing circumstances, as in this example from *Connect 1* (Revell 1990):

> The idea behind this activity is to see what knowledge SS [students] already have of any of Aesop's Fables. If they have absolutely no idea, even after prompting, then cut short this activity and ask them instead to choose one or two of the things and make up a story about them.

An innovative approach to offering teachers alternatives is taken by *New Dimensions 1* (Lonergan and Gordon 1986) in its teacher's book. A right-hand column in the teacher's book is reserved for frequent suggestions on how different activities can be extended or adapted. For instance, the following gives an alternative way of handling the material:

> For a weaker class where there might be too much reading, or simply to make this task more communicative, organize it as Jigsaw Reading.

and this suggests how an exercise can be extended:

> This exercise can be extended so that students ... write the rules for various things such as a school, a hotel, checking in at an airport, driving a car.

This kind of approach is of great value as it provides teachers with new ideas and stimulation and guides those who are less confident towards being more creative and innovative with course material. It also greatly extends what the coursebook offers by way of teaching material, helps to avoid stereotyped teaching and demonstrates sensitivity to learner differences.

Another coursebook which encourages alternatives, this time alternative routes through the material, with a high degree of selectivity, is *The Sourcebook* (Shepherd, Hopkins and Potter 1992), which describes itself as 'the alternative English course'. The intermediate-level teacher's book recognizes that 'every teacher has a different background, training, experience and point of view' and adds that 'each school is a unique entity with ... its own collective attitudes about learning and teaching.' It goes on to offer 'a simple way through the course for those who seek guidance, but practised teachers can play variations on the theme to suit their students, their school and themselves.' An inviting offer indeed!

In general, coursebooks identify the main role of the teacher as that of a guide or facilitator and a monitor. Essentially, the teacher is seen as guiding learners through the learning process, with support from the coursebook, and monitoring student progress, correcting errors when this is useful for the learning process. The teacher's book for *Formula One* (White and Williams 1989) expands on this role:

> The teacher's role is to act as a presenter of material, manager of learning resources and activities, and informant for the students. The teacher will:
> - provide warm-up introductory activities to lead into the lesson;
> - present the new material;
> - provide explanations where needed;
> - direct students to move from one exercise or activity to another;
> - monitor student performance;
> - correct or explain where necessary;
> - encourage personalized application of the language;
> - suggest further practice material from the revision sections and the Workbook.

In the teacher's book for *Campus English* (Forman *et al* 1990), a coursebook specializing in English for Academic Purposes, and therefore at a relatively high language level, there is considerable emphasis on promoting learner independence, and the teacher's role in helping to achieve this:

> It is expected that the teacher's role will be that of monitor and facilitator rather than director. The aim is to promote learner independence from the teacher and students should be encouraged to work without intervention by the teacher [...] The teacher's task is to facilitate the process by which students arrive at an answer.

Here we find a problem-solving approach which encourages students to find their own way through problems, with the support of the teacher where necessary, whose aim is not to give the correct answer but guide students to work out problems themselves in an effective manner, in the process acquiring problem-solving skills which can be transferred to other problem situations without further help from the teacher.

The *monitor* and *guide* model appears to be the commonest, however, in general coursebooks and identifies perhaps the two crucial roles that coursebooks cannot fulfil themselves. This demonstrates that coursebooks have long departed from prescriptive attitudes towards learning and teaching.

Checklist on the teacher's role

☐ Does the coursebook see the teacher's role as that of:
   – guide
   – mentor
   – facilitator
   – manager of learning
   – director
   – monitor?
☐ Does the coursebook recognize the unique function of the teacher in certain aspects of teaching, such as guiding, monitoring and encouraging students, explaining difficulties, responding to questions?
☐ Does the coursebook recognize different learning styles and different teaching styles?
☐ Does the coursebook offer alternatives or ways of extending learning activities?
☐ Does the coursebook promote the development of learner independence (autonomy)?

2   Teachers' books

Most general EFL courses, and some specialized ones, provide teachers' books as part of the whole materials package. They are very important parts of the whole as they can exert a considerable influence on how the course is taught. A good teacher's book is invaluable in offering, among other things, guidelines on how to make the best use of the course, detailed plans for teaching each unit and keys to the exercises. In fact there are a number of possible roles that teachers' books can fulfil, and in principle the more comprehensive they are the better. Teachers' books are likely to have some (and possibly all) of these functions, and we can ask which of them any particular teacher's book fulfils:

- setting out the guiding principles of the course
- stating the aims and objectives of the course
- describing the basis for the selection and grading of the language content
- explaining the rationale for the methodology used
- giving an overview of the way the course is constructed, and of how the different parts relate to one another
- providing practical guidance on how to use the material
- giving linguistic information necessary for effective use of the material in class
- providing background cultural information where this is necessary in order to understand the contexts being used in the material
- promoting better understanding of the principles and practice of language-teaching in general, and helping to develop teaching skills.

It is interesting to note that some teachers' books are written with a more restricted view of their role than others. Some start off with a description of the make-up of the course and then give notes on how to use the contents, unit by unit. Others, with a wider view, consider the principles informing the course and discuss the needs of learners and teachers before focusing on the actual content of the course.

In some parts of the world, where methodology books, professional journals and training courses are unavailable, the teacher's book may be one of the main sources for the professional development of teachers. It is unreasonable to expect a teacher's book to assume the role of a teacher trainer or to substitute entirely for a staff development programme, but any developmental content that it may be able to provide could well have a beneficial result far greater than the writers ever expected. We should certainly look for some element of background theory and practice, and we would hope to find more than just lists of instructions for teachers to carry out.

Anyone writing a teacher's book, particularly one which considers the broader issues just mentioned, has to make difficult assumptions about the existing knowledge of the teachers. Courses written by native speakers for the international market often assume that the teachers will be relatively homogeneous, native speakers or near native speakers themselves, and familiar with the contemporary orthodoxies of TEFL in the western world. So, certain terminology will be used without explanation, because it is assumed to be known to the readers. For example, terms like 'communicative approach' and 'functions' tend to be used without being explained.

It is clearly difficult for the writers of teachers' books, because it would seem pedestrian and patronizing to many teachers if every technical term were explained, yet on the other hand many teachers of English are not native speakers and may not have had the benefit of recent training in TEFL. As Coleman (1985) reminds us, 'the difficulties which the non native speaker teacher of English has to struggle with are frequently underestimated by the writers of ELT materials and by writers on ELT.' The following short extract from the teacher's book for *The Sourcebook Pre-intermediate* (Shepherd and Cox 1991) gives an example of the complexity of language that can be used in teachers' books:

> GRAMMAR FUNCTIONS
> Notes on presentation
> In *The Sourcebook* **Functions** appears as the first section of the **Grammar** part. The aim of the presentations in **Grammar** is to separate and analyse the parts that make up language, and **Functions**, like **Nouns** or **Verbs**, analyses and gives practice in selected areas of language, in this case 10 functional areas, such as 'apologising' and 'inviting'.

A main principle of our approach here is that teachers' books should meet the needs of their users as fully as possible and should be as flexible as possible. Teachers' books should of course whenever possible be pitched appropriately to the level of the users. If they are addressed potentially to a wide range of users, then the needs of the less knowledgeable and confident should not be neglected.

Turning now to more detailed aspects of teachers' books, and in particular to how individual units and items are handled in the teacher's book, we need to check that there are stated objectives for each unit and that sufficiently detailed information is given about language items to be taught. Details of predictable problems that learners may encounter are also very helpful.

A good example of a straightforward but sufficiently detailed explanation of the meaning of a grammar item can be found in connection with the present perfect in *Bridge Plus One Teacher's Manual* (Molteno Project 1987), a course for primary English in South Africa:

> The perfect tense of a verb means an action which was done at a time before writing or speaking the sentence in which it stands, and the results of the action are still effective (present) at the time of writing or speaking.

The strength of such an explanation lies in its simplicity, clarity and intelligibility.

Teachers may appreciate some encouragement when dealing with potentially difficult items like the present perfect, and the teacher's book for *Headway Intermediate* (Soars, J. and L. 1986) offers this supportive comment:

> This use presents problems, as the rule is intangible [...] Do not expect rapid mastery. Students can get very frustrated in their attempts to grapple with this area.

Teachers will expect a teacher's book to provide suggestions for the planning and teaching of lessons. They will seek guidance in what to do and how to do it. We should therefore check that the teacher's book provides suggested procedures for the planning, preparation and teaching of lessons. It is also important that attention is given to the sequencing and progression of lessons and the planning of schemes of work.

Some teachers' books provide a very detailed lesson plan for each unit of material, in some cases even going so far as to specify every activity, including the language to be used by the teacher in class. Further support may be provided by spelling out just what materials and aids are required, sometimes, for example, showing exactly what flashcards, board drawings, etc should look like. Other teachers' books simply provide a small number of sample lesson plans that cover different kinds of activity in the coursebook. In this case it is left to teachers themselves to construct analogous plans for the remaining units. Finally, some teachers' books provide no lesson plans as such, but outline ways of using the different kinds of activity included in the material.

The way guidance is presented in the teacher's book is also important. Are the different sections clear, and can coursebook units be related easily to their corresponding sections in the teacher's book? This can be helped through cross-referencing by page number and by clear page layout. An increasingly popular format is to interleave the pages of the teacher's book into the student's book. The result of this is that the pages of the student's book and the teacher's book always appear next to each other, so that the teacher does not have to fumble about with two separate books at the same time.

An intrinsic part of language teaching concerns evaluating and responding to the language that students produce. Correction techniques are very important, and handled sensitively by the teacher, correction can contribute greatly to effective learning. As we saw earlier, a major role for the teacher is that of monitor, a role that coursebooks cannot fill well. However, teachers' books can give useful advice on the use of correction techniques and can also provide keys to exercises for the benefit of teachers who are not entirely confident of their English. Keys can also give suggested or specimen answers in the case of open-ended tasks where there is no 'correct' answer.

Teachers' books can also offer regular tests which can be used to give students feedback on their progress, and also to give teachers information on which areas of language need to be revised and have yet to be consolidated.

Learner motivation is a major factor in success in language learning and teachers' books can help by providing advice on including sufficient variety of activity in lessons, on using topics of real interest to the learners, on adapting or extending coursebook exercises to match the level and ability of the learners and on being prepared to make quick changes of plan if their interest seems to be flagging. Some extra 'contingency' activities for each unit, which teachers can draw on if necessary, form a valuable addition to the contents of a teacher's book. They can save a lesson that is losing momentum as well as providing teachers with a welcome additional sense of security.

One suggestion for future teachers' books, as I have not found it included in any of those I surveyed, is that a blank space should be left at the end of each section or unit, for noting down any additional ideas that have come up whilst planning or teaching the lesson. Evaluative comments on lessons taught could also be noted down there, particularly if the comments related to ways of using the material, so that they could be reviewed the next time the same unit was taught.

Checklist for teachers' books

- ☐ How comprehensive and flexible is the teacher's book?
- ☐ Is it written so as to be comprehensible to less experienced teachers?
- ☐ Is it suitable for native and non-native speaker teachers?
- ☐ Is the underlying approach of the writers expressed clearly and explicitly, or does it have to be inferred?
- ☐ Does the teacher's book provide enough detailed information on the language items to be taught?
- ☐ Does the teacher's book give enough guidance on the teaching procedures advocated?
- ☐ Is there enough cultural explanation to enable teachers unfamiliar with, for example, British lifestyles to interpret and exploit appropriately the situations portrayed in the coursebook?
- ☐ How prescriptive is the guidance provided (bearing in mind that a moderately prescriptive approach may be appropriate when teacher expectations require it)?
- ☐ Are there clear objectives for each unit/lesson?
- ☐ Are new language items explained intelligibly in terms of their form and meaning/use?
- ☐ Are there outline plans for each unit/lesson?
- ☐ Are teaching procedures clearly explained?
- ☐ Are learning difficulties predicted and appropriate advice given?
- ☐ How detailed is the information and advice given?
- ☐ Is the same detail given for every unit, or only for sample units?
- ☐ Can the contents of the teacher's book be related easily to the relevant sections of the student's book?
- ☐ Is advice given on informal monitoring of students and on using correction techniques?
- ☐ Are keys to exercises and other activities provided?
- ☐ Are there regular progress tests and advice on when and how to use them, and how to follow them up?
- ☐ Does the teacher's book make a positive contribution to heightening and sustaining learner motivation?
- ☐ Are teachers encouraged to note down their own ideas in the teacher's book?
- ☐ Are there any guidelines for evaluating how well lessons went?

Chapter 10 Communicative coursebooks

1   Aims of communicative language teaching

Communicative language teaching has become the accepted orthodoxy of TEFL over the past ten years or more, and many, but not all, general courses refer to communicative goals, communicative practice or communicative methodology. *Blueprint One* (Abbs and Freebairn 1990), for example, highlights the students' need to communicate effectively: 'Students need to know that the language they are going to learn will enable them to communicate their needs, ideas and opinions. Motivation ... comes from knowing that language activities in the classroom are at all times meaningful and aimed at real-life communication.' *The New Cambridge English Course* (Swan and Walter 1990) recommends that 'language practice should resemble real-life communication, with genuine exchange of information and opinions', whilst *Formula One* (White and Williams 1989) aims at 'providing ... an ability to use the language for communicative purposes' and *Grapevine* (Viney, P. and K. 1990) gives as one of its first principles 'an emphasis on communicative goals'.

Flying Colours (Garton-Sprenger and Greenall 1991) gives 'communicative aims' for all of its lessons and these are expressed as a mixture of communicative activities and language functions in terms such as the following:

> Giving instructions
> Describing a sequence of actions
> Criticising
> Expressing obligation.

Headway Intermediate (Soars, J. and L. 1986) in its teacher's book outlines usefully what in its view communicative methodology amounts to:

> *Headway* incorporates and encourages what is generally considered to be a *communicative methodology*:
> – Students are challenged cognitively.
> – They are involved in the learning process.
> – They are asked to contribute their own opinions, experiences and feelings.
> – They take part in real or realistic activities.
> – They are encouraged to work closely with peers.
> – They are encouraged to assume a certain responsibility for their own learning, and to develop learning skills.
> – The teacher adopts differing roles (informer, monitor, resource consultant) according to the stage of the lesson.

Richards and Rodgers (1986) consider communicative language teaching to be (in their terminology) an *approach* rather than a *method*. The distinction that they are making is that there is no one accepted methodology for communicative language teaching: it can be carried out in different ways, and its breadth and comprehensive nature make it bigger in scope than other approaches and methods: 'There is no single text or authority on it, nor any single model that is universally accepted as authoritative.' Its aims, according to Richards and Rodgers, are twofold: 'to make communicative competence the goal of language teaching and to develop procedures for the teaching of the four language skills that acknowledge the interdependence of language and communication.'

Its theoretical base, again according to Richards and Rodgers, includes these characteristics:

1. Language is a system for the expression of meaning.
2. The primary function of language is for interaction and communication.
3. The structure of language reflects its functional and communicative uses.
4. The primary units of language are not merely its grammatical and structural features, but categories of functional and communicative meaning as exemplified in discourse.

2 Communicative coursebooks: design and content

Realizing some of these theoretical principles in course materials is not necessarily an easy thing to do, particularly when there are other competing criteria that have to be taken into account, such as giving a thorough, well-graded grounding in grammar. Moreover, as we have seen, course materials of different kinds can be communicative in different ways. A general coursebook can include interactions that display some features of real-life communication, a book of roleplays can set up realistic situations in which learners can communicate, material focusing on the written language can set up realistic activities involving reading and writing. All of these can be regarded as communicative to a greater or lesser extent.

It is an open question to what extent coursebooks can include *real* communicative activities, but at most levels it is possible to include *realistic* activities, often based on contrived information gaps of various kinds, which involve, at the least, language use which is communicative in the context of the classroom. Examples of these are jigsaw reading and jigsaw listening, which are useful activities for promoting communicative language use, but are not based on commonly occurring real-life communication situations.

When evaluating such activities, we must consider to what extent the skills and strategies learned and practised are transferable to the real world. In general, the greater the potential for transfer, the more valuable the activity. So, for example, jigsaw listening and reading could be seen as useful preparation for real-life situations in which individuals needed to share partial information on a subject with others who had different information, in order to pool knowledge and form a more complete picture of the subject in question.

Littlewood (1981) distinguishes helpfully between *quasi-communicative activities, functional communication activities*, and *social interaction activities*, each being a stage more communicative than the one before it. Significantly, it is at the level of social interaction that complex factors, such as the structuring of discourse and the strategic planning of communication, come into play and demonstrate the importance of preparing learners for the active and dynamic process of participating in the creation of genuine discourse. How far removed this is from participating in predetermined coursebook dialogues is not always recognized, and the additional skills required to operate effectively are often overlooked, perhaps understandably, as they are only sketchily described and understood at the present state of our knowledge. We will look at this important area in more detail later in this chapter.

A more rigorous approach to evaluating materials in terms of their contribution to communicative language teaching would be to analyse in all their complexity the sorts of real-life interactions that students would be expected to participate in and match them against the models and practice activities incorporated in the materials. One of the main problems that coursebook writers encounter in attempting to replicate genuine communication is its intrinsic unpredictability and relative complexity. Transactional interactions such as service encounters *are* predictable to a certain degree in their unmarked forms, but even here the precise route taken by any one interaction cannot be predicted accurately. Indeed if it could be predicted totally, there would be no need for the interaction to take place, except possibly for phatic purposes, as the participants would know the outcome before it had even begun. Consequently we must regard unpredictability as an inherent characteristic of communicative interaction and look at how coursebooks equip learners to handle it, both productively and receptively.

The structure of interactions of a transactional nature has been shown to be rather more complex than coursebooks would lead us to believe. For example, simple question-and-answer sequences, which are commonplace in coursebooks, rarely take place in reality. Even straightforward transactional interactions include openers, pre-closers, hesitations and insertion sequences, which are rarely found in coursebook dialogues. We will review some research evidence on this later in this chapter.

Checklist for communicative coursebooks: design and content

- ☐ Does the coursebook claim to be communicative in its aims?
- ☐ Are specific communicative aims or objectives indicated, either generally or in connection with individual units?
- ☐ Is the syllabus of the coursebook primarily communicative (eg by using communicative activities, functions, etc as its primary units)?
- ☐ Is there reference to communicative methodology?
- ☐ Is there evidence that the design of the coursebook is influenced by communicative considerations (eg emphasis given to communicative activities, use of authentic materials and realistic tasks)?
- ☐ If communicative activities are used as learning material, are they *real*, in terms of the real world, or *realistic*, ie communicative in the classroom situation only?
- ☐ Do *realistic* activities promote the learning of communicative skills and strategies which are transferable to real-life communication?

3   The element of unpredictability: case study

As coursebooks are written products, designed and produced in advance of their use, it is extremely difficult to inject the crucial element of unpredictability into the interactions that they contain. More sophisticated technologies, such as interactive video, may be better equipped to handle this aspect of language use, and it will be interesting in the future to observe how their potential is exploited by materials writers and designers. Some early steps have already been taken, but there is probably much scope for further development.

At present, however, the vast majority of learners and teachers do not have access to either the hardware or software necessary, and we must still rely on the coursebook as our main source of material. In this area teachers do seem to have an even more important role to play than usual in ensuring that classroom interactions are not unnecessarily stereotyped and predictable. Let us see how coursebooks can help to achieve this through providing communicative exercises and activities, focusing on spoken interaction, an area where handling unpredictability is particularly important, as real-time constraints come into play and learners have to understand and respond in a matter of seconds.

Straight dialogues for listening and repetition are becoming rarer in coursebooks, but they are still found, either in the form shown in the example below from *Grapevine 1* (Viney, P. and K. 1990), or in strip cartoon form. In either case individual dialogues may stand alone or may form part of an on-going story, as in the case of the example from *Grapevine*:

1
Stacey What's the time?
Lambert Eleven thirty.
Stacey They're late.
Lambert Yeah . . . or we're early.
Stacey Listen . . . what's that?
Lambert It's a car. Is it their car?
Stacey Yeah, it is. Come on . . .

2
Stacey Hi!
1st Man Hi. Where's the picture?
Stacey The Picasso.
1st Man Yeah, yeah, the Picasso. Where is it?
Stacey It's in the briefcase. Where are the diamonds?
1st Man They're in the bag.
Stacey Where is the bag?
2nd Man It's in our car.
Stacey
1st Man } Get the bag!

From *Grapevine 1*, Viney, P. and K. (OUP 1990)

Students are expected to listen and understand, to do some selective repetition, to read the dialogue silently and to read it in pairs. At a later stage, the dialogue forms the basis for a roleplay activity, where the content of the dialogue is recreated from memory. It will be seen that, although this is sound language practice, there is very little that could be called communicative if we include unpredictability as a central feature of communicative interaction, since the dialogue is entirely predetermined, and the student activities are equally preordained.

A rather different activity, also from *Grapevine 1*, shows how a limited but genuine element of unpredictability can be introduced into oral work by having students ask and answer questions about their own likes and dislikes:

---

1 Ask another student questions.
A *Do you like football?*
B *Yes, I do. / No, I don't.*
Put a tick [✔] for yes, and a cross [✗] for no.

2 Work with a different student.
A *Does she like football?*
B *Yes, she does. / No, she doesn't.*
Talk about the answers in 1 above.

3 Work with the same student.
A *Which sports do you like?*
B *I like football and tennis. I don't like swimming.*
Ask and answer.

4 Work with a different student.
A *Which sports does he like?*
B *He likes football and tennis. He doesn't like swimming.*
Talk about the answers in 3 above.

From *Grapevine 1*, Viney, P. and K. (OUP 1990)

As the level is still elementary, we would not expect to see a high level of unpredictability, but just enough to make the interaction meaningful and to start to give students the experience of coping with language use that is open-ended.

The example on p 121 from *The New Cambridge English Course 1* (Swan and Walter 1990) shows a progression from a set dialogue in Exercise 2 through a gapped dialogue in Exercise 3 (with a complete version on cassette) to Exercise 4, consisting of instructions to students to make up similar conversations based on the earlier dialogues. Only Exercise 4 has an element of unpredictability, as the other two exercises are made up of pre-written dialogues. Such a progression is useful, as it leads learners on from predictable and invariable models of dialogues to situations where the content and direction of the interaction are not entirely predetermined.

5C Where's the nearest post office?

> Asking for and giving directions.

1 Put the words with the correct pictures.

> phone box   supermarket   bank   post office
> police station   car park   bus stop   station

1 post office

2

3

4

5

6

7

8

2 Listen and practise these dialogues.

A: Excuse me. Where's the nearest post office, please?
B: It's over there on the [right] / [left.]
A: Oh, thank you very much.
B: Not at all.

      *   *   *

A: Excuse me. Where's the nearest bank, please?
B: I'm sorry, I don't know.
A: Thank you anyway.

3 🔊 Complete these dialogues and practise them.

A: .... the manager's office,
.... ?
B: .... by the reception desk.
A: ....

      *   *   *

A: .... the toilets,
.... ?
B: Upstairs .... the first floor, first door ....
.... left.
A: .... much.

4 Make up similar conversations in pairs and practise them. You are: a person who lives in your town and a foreign tourist; or a visitor to your school and a student; or a visitor to the planet Mars and a Martian.

> **Learn:** there; over there; right; left; on the right/left; Thank you anyway; Not at all; by; upstairs; downstairs.
>
> **Learn four or more:** phone box; supermarket; bank; post office; police; police station; car park; bus stop; station.

26

From *The New Cambridge English Course 1*, Swan and Walter (CUP 1990)

Substitution dialogues have a long history, and, while not truly communicative, can still be useful at the quasi-communicative stage, where the building blocks of communicative interaction are being learned. This example from *Formula One* (White and Williams 1989) is typical:

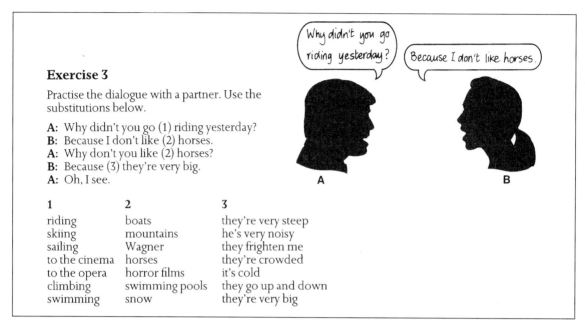

Exercise 3

Practise the dialogue with a partner. Use the substitutions below.

A: Why didn't you go (1) riding yesterday?
B: Because I don't like (2) horses.
A: Why don't you like (2) horses?
B: Because (3) they're very big.
A: Oh, I see.

1	2	3
riding	boats	they're very steep
skiing	mountains	he's very noisy
sailing	Wagner	they frighten me
to the cinema	horses	they're crowded
to the opera	horror films	it's cold
climbing	swimming pools	they go up and down
swimming	snow	they're very big

From *Formula One*, White and Williams (Macmillan 1989)

It is interesting in one respect because, paradoxically, it incorporates significant elements of unpredictability (for example, student B's response in line 2 of the dialogue will depend on what student A says in line 1, and cannot be formulated in advance) without being genuinely communicative, because the students are not necessarily saying things which are true for them. Rather they are doing a sort of elaborate substitution table.

The example on p 123 from *Flying Colours 2* (Garton-Sprenger and Greenall 1991) shows how controlled interactions can also be genuinely communicative, as here students are encouraged to talk about their own experiences.

However, the structure of the conversations shown is very simple and, except in Exercise 8, the quick unpredictable responses characteristic of real conversations are not practised.

7 Work in pairs. Ask and say what you have done.

		the Pompidou Centre Venezuela Spain
	seen . . . ?	*Coming Home* the Arctic
Have you	read . . . ?	*Love in the Time of Cholera* Mexico
	been to . . . ?	*Klute* Antarctica the Lloyds Building
		One Hundred Years of Solitude Paris

8 Ask your partner about other books, films, places and buildings.

A Have you read *The Name of the Rose*?
B No, I haven't read it yet, but I've seen the film.

A Have you ever been to Hong Kong?
B Yes, I have. It's a very exciting place.

A Have you seen the Parthenon?
B No, I've never been to Greece.

9 Ask other students about their experiences and note down their answers.

Have you ever . . . ?

lived abroad	worked in a bar or a restaurant
been to another continent	used a computer
been in a play or a film	played in a band or an orchestra
written a poem or a story	been on TV
won a prize	flown a plane
worked in a shop	ridden a horse

10 Write sentences using the information you have collected.

Paulo has worked in a bar, but he hasn't worked in a restaurant.
Cristina has been to Australia, but she's never lived abroad.
No one has ever flown a plane.

From *Flying Colours 2*, Garton-Sprenger and Greenall (Heinemann 1991)

An interesting model of a simple simulation which injects unpredictability into the interaction is this, from *Blueprint One* (Abbs and Freebairn 1990):

---

7 WRITING

Imagine that you lose a valuable possession, e.g. a ring, a watch, or an address book. Write a form like the one below on to a piece of paper.

LOST
Item(s): A watch
Description: Gold, with a black strap
Where left or lost: In sports centre
When: On Monday 21st January

8 ROLEPLAY

Distribute the 'forms' around the class so that nobody knows whose they have got. In turn, say what you have found. The owner must prove that it belongs to him/ her by answering your questions correctly. Use the questions from Exercise 6 to help you.

A: I've found a watch. Whose is it?
B: I think it's mine.
A: What . . .?
B: . . .
A: O.K. It's yours./No, it isn't yours.

From *Blueprint One*, Abbs and Freebairn (Longman 1990)

Here, although the 'lost' items in Exercise 7 are imaginary, they are made up by the students themselves, probably based on objects that they do own, and therefore will have more reality to the students than items imposed by the coursebook. It is yet another example of an activity which, like the others that we have already seen, incorporates some aspects of genuine communicative interaction, but not all of them. Perhaps this is as much as we can expect a coursebook to do, as there will always be a jump to be made from the learning situation to the real world outside.

One useful way of making the coursebook activity closer to real life is to replace the dialogue with a set of instructions which, if followed, will allow two or more students working together to create a conversation. Here they are told what to say, but not how to say it. So the activity is not wholly communicative, as the students are saying what they have been told to say and not what they themselves have decided to say. But it is very valuable practice in the creation of spoken discourse and brings into play factors such as strategic planning of communication, the structuring of longer stretches of discourse and the co-operative element necessary for the effective exchange of meaning and the understanding of speakers' intentions.

In the example below from *Discoveries 2* (Abbs and Freebairn 1986), students have to formulate their own language but the meaning of each turn is known to both speakers in advance. Therefore the discourse-creation element is limited to the level of language form, eg using suitable linking and reference devices, as the answers to the questions asked are already known and can be learned by simply looking at the instructions for the next turn.

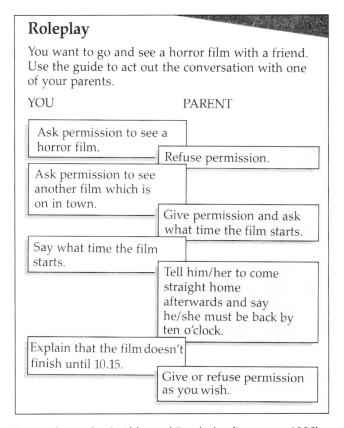

Roleplay

You want to go and see a horror film with a friend. Use the guide to act out the conversation with one of your parents.

YOU	PARENT
Ask permission to see a horror film.	
	Refuse permission.
Ask permission to see another film which is on in town.	
	Give permission and ask what time the film starts.
Say what time the film starts.	
	Tell him/her to come straight home afterwards and say he/she must be back by ten o'clock.
Explain that the film doesn't finish until 10.15.	
	Give or refuse permission as you wish.

From *Discoveries 2*, Abbs and Freebairn (Longman 1986)

The element of unpredictability, though not the opportunity for students to say what they want, is built in to the cue cards activity from *Cambridge Advanced English* (Jones 1991) that we looked at in Chapter 6 (p 69) by the simple expedient of separating out the instructions to the different students participating, and putting them on different pages in the back of the book. Each student only looks at his/her own set of instructions and therefore cannot see what the others are going to say. In this way good practice is given in both expressing oneself and responding quickly and effectively to what others say, whilst providing the framework for a fairly controlled interaction.

4   Coursebook language and real-life language use

As coursebooks exist to prepare learners to use English independently in the real world, it is justifiable to compare the models of language use that they provide with samples of real-life language use in so far as they can be obtained. A very interesting study in this area of research has been reported by Scotton and Bernsten (1988) who undertook some empirical work specifically to see if coursebook dialogues were representative of real-life language use in two common interaction situations: asking the way in the street and making requests in service encounters at a post office and at a university information desk.

Naturally occurring conversations were recorded and analysed and then compared with typical corresponding coursebook dialogues. It was found that, within the same situation type, the overall discourse structure was remarkably similar in all instances of conversations recorded, but that there was variation of semantic content and lexical choices. The striking findings of the research, however, were that the structure of naturally-occurring conversation was *not* reflected in the coursebook dialogues that were studied. Two contrasting examples from the research will illustrate this point. The first is a dialogue from an American coursebook, *Notion by Notion* (Ferreira 1981), and the second is a natural conversation recorded at Michigan State University.

Coursebook dialogue

S1: Excuse me, how can I get to the post office from here?
S2: Cross University Avenue. Turn right. Walk straight ahead along University Avenue for three blocks. Turn left at Church Street. Walk south for two blocks. Turn left at Avenue. The post office is the big building on the corner of Bridge Avenue and Church Street.
S1: Thank you for your help.

Natural conversation

S1: How do I get to the Vet Clinic?
S2: Oh, my God. It's far, but, um. It's on, it's Shaw Lane is right, if you keep going up here you'll hit Shaw Lane and it's going that way. But go a little bit more and then cross the parking lot and it goes that way.
S1: Um hum.
S2: And then cross the road and just follow the sidewalk all the way down. If you keep following it you'll see a sign that says Vet Clinic. But go all the way down there and cross the road and just follow the sidewalk down.
S1: Okay.
S2: Okay?
S1: Thanks a lot.

As can be seen, the real conversation is much less 'well formed' in that it contains hesitations, fillers and incomplete sentences. All these features are of course typical of spoken language produced by native speakers. It is also significant that in the study 96 per cent of responses to the request for directions did not begin by actually giving directions, but started with an opener of some kind, like the one in the example above. This opener then finished with a 'readiness marker' indicating that the directions themselves were about to begin. This usually took the form of a pause or a filler, such as *um* or *OK*.

The form of the directions themselves is predictable but shows more variation in type than in coursebook dialogues. The preferred choice is the bald imperative, but over 74 per cent of speakers used more than one type and over 51 per cent used three or more types. These included *you* + verb (eg *you go*), *you* + auxiliary + main verb (eg *you want to go up this street*) and indirect types such as *The best way to go would be to ...*

Although they would not use exactly the kind of natural conversation that we have just seen, in this context coursebooks should equip learners to understand a wider range of ways of giving directions than is found in average dialogues. In addition the research suggests that learners will need more language to request directions than simply an initial request and a final *thank you*. This is because the direction-givers required confirmation that their directions were being understood and asked orientation checkers requiring yes/no answers or longer responses within the body of the conversation.

The implications for learners include the following:

- they need to recognize markers which distinguish the central parts of the interaction from the peripheral parts, such as openers, pre-closers, etc
- they need to be able to edit out fillers, pauses, etc
- they need to recognize and understand a fairly wide range of structures (not just imperatives)
- they need to interact with the interlocutor throughout the exchange, responding to confirmation and orientation checkers.

The more general implication for evaluating coursebooks is that we cannot afford to lose sight of real-life language use, and even if we do not have research results to guide us, we can at least make use of our own observations to judge whether coursebook material provides a good model for equipping learners to communicate effectively.

5 The organization of conversation

The research evidence that we have looked at above highlights some of the features of natural conversations that are not always reproduced in coursebooks. A number of other features of conversations which have been identified by research in conversational analysis (CA) are worth considering in relation to the models given in coursebooks.

One of the basic units of conversation is the *turn* and *turn-taking* is an essential skill for anyone who wants to take part in conversation. The fact that turn-taking occurs with split-second timing between two or more people illustrates the collaborative nature of conversation and suggests that there are rules and conventions for turn-taking which are shared by all members of a speech community.

The conventions are not yet fully understood, but some significant features have been identified which are relevant to language teaching. First, there are certain points in a conversation (perhaps at the end of a main clause) where other speakers can come in and where the current speaker is most vulnerable to interruption. Second, where interruption does occur, the current speaker has the right to nominate who speaks next. Third, he or she can do this by using a combination of linguistic, paralinguistic and kinesic cues, such as addressing the nominated speaker by name, or by the use of eye contact. Coursebooks interested in equipping learners communicatively could provide models of and practice in turn-taking and interruption techniques. This could include identifying places where the next speaker can come in, whether nominated or not, learning ways of nominating the next speaker, and learning suitable formulae for interrupting. The real-time constraints inherent in turn-taking have already been discussed earlier in this chapter.

A further way of helping learners to perceive the patterns of conversation organization is to focus on *adjacency pairs* – paired utterances such as question–answer, offer–acceptance, request–compliance. Such adjacency pairs seem to be a fundamental unit of conversation organization. Practice with typical adjacency pairs in short realistic dialogues will help learners in prediction skills and develop their ability to respond in real time. Coursebooks do include adjacency pairs in their dialogues and conversations, but as always we should look carefully to see how well they reflect natural conversations.

It is an oversimplification to suggest that conversations are just made up of sequences of adjacency pairs, but they are useful building blocks for learning conversational skills. A rather more complex structure is produced when *framing* occurs. In this case *insertion sequences*, usually adjacency pairs themselves, are placed between the first and second part of an adjacency pair, as in this example:

```
 ┌─A: Where did you get this wine from?
 │ ┌─B: Do you like it?
 │ │ ┌─A: I expect it was expensive.
 │ │ └─B: Not at all!
 │ └─A: Yes it's good.
 └─B: Well, it was only from the supermarket on the corner.
```

As we can see, there are two insertions here, making it a little more complex, but more real than the majority of coursebook dialogues. Students should have little difficulty in handling such multiple insertion sequences at intermediate or advanced levels, as they are likely to occur in their mother tongues and transfer will be straightforward.

A final aspect of conversation organization that we might consider is that of *preferred sequences*. In the context of requesting or getting others to do something, the preferred sequence in English is for A to elicit an offer from B, rather than for A to make a direct request to B. The following is an example of a preferred sequence:

C: Hello, I was just ringing up to ask if you were going to Bertrand's party.
R: Yes, I thought you might be.
C: Heh heh.
R: Yes, would you like a lift?
C: Oh I'd love one.
R: Right okay um I'll pick you up from there.
(Levinson 1983 p 359)

In this context, we might look for teaching material which equips learners to elicit an offer as a first strategy when trying to get another person to do something, and only to make a request if the attempt fails.

In materials for developing communicative abilities in spoken English, we should above all be looking for an awareness that interactions are collaborative activities involving two or more people competing for the floor and negotiating meaning. The discourse is dynamic, being created by the speakers and developing sequentially in time. Therefore it is subject to real-time constraints, is relatively unpredictable and is certainly not a pre-determined series of perfectly formed sentences.

Some interesting comments on fluency based on the results of empirical studies by Sajvaara and Lehtonen (1978) emphasize the importance of the aspects of interactions that we have just looked at: 'It is not the good language competence that is an indicator of fluency, but the perception of the hearer, what sort of attitudes various elements in a speaker's performance trigger in the hearer.' On the basis of the study, grammatically correct sentences do not constitute fluency: native speakers who produced more examples of false starts, incomplete sentences, rephrasings, etc than foreign speakers were nevertheless perceived to speak more fluently than the foreign speakers whose language was well formed and grammatically correct.

Checklist for communicative interactions

- [ ] What elements of genuine communication are present:
  - unpredictability
  - opportunities to express real information, feelings, opinions, etc
  - opportunities for learners to structure their own discourse
  - need to formulate and use communication strategies
  - emphasis on co-operation between speakers in communicative interaction?
- [ ] At the appropriate level, does the coursebook include material that reflects the nature of communicative interaction, in respect of:
  - structure of discourse in interactions (including openers, confirmation checkers, pre-closers, etc)
  - complexity of structure
  - range of appropriate lexis
  - features such as fillers and incomplete sentences
  - roles of speakers in interactions?
- [ ] Does the material help learners in the skill of turn-taking in conversations?
- [ ] Are adjacency pairs included in presentation and practice material? If so, are there examples of framing (insertion sequences)?
- [ ] Are there examples of preferred sequences (eg eliciting an offer rather than making a direct request)?
- [ ] Is any other help given with the organization and structuring of conversations or other spoken interactions?

6   Style and appropriacy

Learners need to develop a sensitivity to stylistic variation in order to participate effectively in spoken interactions. The range of variation does not have to be as wide as that of a native speaker, but there should be an awareness of and a sensitivity to differences between informal, neutral and formal styles of speech. This awareness and sensitivity should be linked to a recognition of the types of speech situation where different levels of formality are appropriate. As we saw when considering style and appropriacy in Chapter 4, the concept of communicative competence includes the ability to perceive the social situations in which language is being used and select and use the style (formal, informal, etc) appropriate to each particular situation. Matching style to situation is important, particularly as the choice of the wrong style (eg informal style in a formal business meeting or formal style in a family situation) can send the wrong message and cause offence.

Learners will already use different degrees of formality in their own languages, so there is a foundation to build on, and coursebooks can help enormously by presenting examples of different styles in English in their appropriate contexts and identifying some of the main characteristics of formal and informal English. Once learners reach intermediate level there is scope for them to become gradually sensitized to stylistic variation and equipped both to recognize and produce a moderate range of different stylistic features, linked to situations in which they would be used.

At a more advanced level, students should be helped as far as possible to internalize some of the underlying principles which determine where a particular utterance lies on a formality scale. This will give learners a fuller understanding of the use of stylistic variation than just learning some set phrases, and will ultimately allow them to vary quite substantially in terms of style the language that they use in different kinds of interactions.

The most important variables that come into play in the speech situation are:

- the physical context (setting)
- the social roles of the participants *in that context*
- the goals of the participants (the purpose of the interaction).

If we take the example of making requests, or, to give a broader definition, getting others to do things, we see that the utterances used will vary on a sliding scale along at least two axes. The first axis is that of relative social roles in the context of the interaction: the greater the social distance, the more formal the style. The second axis concerns the speaker's goal, in this case whether the speaker is trying to get the other person to perform a small task or a large task. Leech (1983) refers to this as the *cost–benefit* scale. The greater the cost to the other person, the more formal (polite) is the style of the speaker.

If a coursebook presents a number of examples which can be used to make requests and grades them on a 'politeness scale' with, at one extreme, *Shut the door*, and, at the other, *Could you possibly shut the door, please*, this will be of some help to learners. However, such a presentation gives isolated exponents of a particular function, without a context and without a principled explanation of *why* one is more polite than another. Two more things can be done. First, the examples need to be integrated into a realistic piece of discourse, such as a dialogue which will both provide context in terms of social roles, goals, etc and will demonstrate the examples in use within the collaborative framework of the dialogue. Second, in order to be able to generate appropriately formulated requests rather than simply repeat phrases learned parrot fashion, students need to understand why some utterances are more polite or formal than others.

In the case of making requests, this can be explained relatively straightforwardly in terms of the speaker giving the hearer the opportunity to refuse without giving offence or losing face. This can best be done by claiming that it is not possible to accede to the request, ie that the hearer is *unable* rather than *unwilling* to agree. So, an indirect request which questions the hearer's ability (rather than willingness) to comply is considered more polite. In this exchange:

A: Would you be able to give me a lift to the party tonight?
B: I'm awfully sorry but I can't because I've already got a car-full.

A gives B the opportunity to refuse, on the grounds that he or she is unable to do it, through the way in which the request is formulated. An alternative request in a more direct (informal) style, such as *Please give me a lift to the party tonight* or *Do give me a lift to the party tonight* is more difficult to refuse politely, but of course if the participants in the interaction are already well acquainted, a more direct refusal such as *Sorry, not tonight* will not necessarily cause offence. The concept of *optionality*, how easy the speaker makes it for the other person to refuse, should not be a difficult one for learners to grasp and may well be directly transferable from their own languages. In any case it is simpler than many grammatical concepts.

Coursebooks which have a communicative aim can be expected to give some attention to matters of style and we should check if they do so.

Checklist for style and appropriacy

☐ Is there material for sensitizing learners to different levels of formality?
☐ If so, are the examples presented sufficiently contextualized?
☐ Is the level of formality related to the setting, social roles of the participants and their communicative goals?
☐ Is practice given in using different levels of formality in different situations?
☐ Are learners led towards an understanding of why some forms in English are more formal than others?
☐ Are any other aspects of style other than formality/informality included (eg register – the language used within a particular activity or occupation)?

Chapter 11 ESP materials

Teaching materials for English for Specific Purposes (ESP) tend to be viewed as distinct and separate from general coursebooks. This may be because of the emphasis on content and the unfamiliarity of the content to many teachers. There are also differences in the roles of teachers and learners and in the design of the materials. For these reasons, we need to keep some additional considerations in mind when selecting ESP materials.

1 Characteristics of ESP materials

To those who are uninitiated into the rather esoteric world of ESP, the approach and materials can seem unfamiliar and inaccessible. However, this is a misleading impression probably created by the specialized and often technical nature of the subject content in ESP books. The range of ESP books on the market is large and covers many disciplines and occupations from medicine to banking, from physics to tourism and from law to aviation. The three areas best catered for by published material in Britain are English for business, English for science and technology (EST) and English for academic purposes (EAP).

Although the content of ESP books may look very different from that of general coursebooks, and the skills being developed may have a different balance from those in general coursebooks, the guidelines for the evaluation of materials which were discussed in Chapter 2 also apply to ESP materials. We should check that ESP materials meet learners' needs and that the language taught matches the language that the students will use. The material should take into account learner expectations and learning styles and should have a clear role in the learning/teaching process.

So far as meeting learners' needs is concerned, ESP materials have sometimes been in advance of general coursebooks, as they have been developed specially for students who were perceived to have specific needs which could not be met fully by general material. These needs were originally seen mainly in terms of subject content. So, for example, engineers need the language of engineering, doctors the language of medicine, pilots the language of aviation, etc, and this is indeed the case. However, as the subject content becomes defined more narrowly, so the number of different areas proliferates. For example, in my own experience of teaching on a study-skills course, we had a grouping of students who were preparing to study 'life sciences' at postgraduate level. This is already a sub-division of science, but we found increasing levels of sub-division into botany, zoology, ecology, etc. And within ecology we had one plant ecologist and one animal ecologist!

Clearly it is beyond the bounds of possibility for published materials to cope specifically with distinctions which seem so fine to us, but which are fundamental to specialists in their own fields. To some extent teachers on ESP courses can supplement the published material available by producing their own materials, perhaps based on specialized texts. However, this is very time-consuming and normally only small quantities of such individualized material can be produced during a course.

The solution to this problem most commonly adopted is to work within broader subject areas such as science, engineering, medicine, etc, whilst at the same time focusing on the skills, strategies and abilities that learners need in order to operate effectively in their discipline in English. Scientific language, for example, will display common features in its use of grammar, its range of vocabulary and its discourse structure. At the same time students studying the subject at university level will need to learn to perform specific tasks through language, such as reading academic articles, listening to lectures and taking notes, and participating in seminar discussions. Students are thus equipped to handle the broad features of scientific language and are also equipped with the sets of skills and strategies necessary to use this language in their subsequent academic studies.

The same general approach holds for other areas of ESP, such as business. In this case students might learn the specific language features found in the business context (eg letters, invoices, tenders, reports) and at the same time become equipped to use this language in negotiating, making presentations, dictating letters, etc.

Once this firm foundation is laid, very specialized language can be learned with the help of a small amount of very specialized material produced in-house, and in many cases the students concerned, being the experts in the subject, can make a contribution to the material and can undertake a considerable amount of individual study.

In evaluating ESP material we should look at both the 'core' specialist language and at the skills and strategies taught. We also need to check if there is a good balance between the two.

2   Student and teacher roles

At the level of much ESP work, the roles of teachers and learners will be different from those in general courses. They will be more equal in most cases, partly because ESP students tend to be older and already established in their professions, but also because the students have crucial subject knowledge that the teacher does not have. English language teachers cannot be expected to have specialist knowledge outside their own field. If they do, then it is a happy coincidence. But the range of ESP subject areas is so large that it is unrealistic to expect that there will always be a teacher available with the necessary specialist knowledge.

Consequently a useful and often fruitful partnership can be developed between teacher and students, where they pool their knowledge and expertise to produce an effective course. One main advantage of this, apart from the obvious one of remedying the teacher's lack of specialist knowledge, is that students feel more involved in the course and have a greater stake in it.

ESP materials can encourage this kind of collaborative relationship. We should look for an approach which makes use of the combined knowledge and expertise of teachers and students working together.

3   Design and methodology

In design, ESP materials may differ considerably from general coursebooks. For one thing, they will generally assume a foundation of proficiency in general English, and from the start will focus on aspects of English specific to the subject area being covered. Similarly, the balance of language skills being taught may be different from that found in general courses. In some cases, there may be a strong emphasis on the written language and oral skills may be totally ignored; in other cases the material may focus on very specific skills, such as note-taking from a talk, presentation or lecture.

Flexibility in use is a particularly valuable asset in ESP materials, as there may be very special constraints operating in the learning/teaching situation. For example, in a business context learners may be extremely busy in their work and may also be subject to unexpected demands on their time, leading to sporadic attendance or an irregular study pattern. Material which can accommodate this will be more effective than material that cannot. A modular design, with each unit being as self-contained as possible, allows learners to continue to study effectively even when several lessons have been missed. Materials which can be used for individual study whenever time is available will also be advantageous, allowing learners to cover the ground of any lessons missed and to work independently on material which is particularly relevant to their needs. An ESP coursebook which doubles as a sourcebook is valuable in this context, particularly when it is accompanied by material on cassette which can be listened to, for example, in a car.

Methodologically, the general principles which apply to general coursebooks also apply to ESP materials. Additionally, we might expect to see an emphasis on the development of specific skills and strategies for operating in the ESP context. This can be done by the use of skill-based and task-based activities involving an element of problem solving and drawing substantially for their content on the learners' specialist subject knowledge and professional experience. Project work which replicates real-life situations is an effective way of helping learners to develop the skills and strategies that they will need. The co-operation necessary for a group project will also give learners the opportunity to develop their language skills in inter-personal relations and will help to give them confidence in using English professionally.

The balance and mix of skills that the students need will be represented naturally in the projects undertaken, so long as they in turn are representative of the professional situations in which the students operate. Working backwards from the projects and tasks selected, ESP materials writers can then produce preparatory material that the learners will go through before undertaking a particular task or project.

A further advantage of a task-based approach is that, at the end, there is a product of a realistic nature. This not only gives learners a feeling of achievement, but also gives them the opportunity to evaluate their performance against real-world criteria which they themselves will have, based on their previous professional experience.

Checklist for ESP materials

☐ Is the material based on a careful analysis of learner needs?
☐ Are objectives specified:
  – in content terms
  – in performance terms?
☐ Is the content appropriate to learners' needs? Does it have credibility (face validity)?
☐ Is there a body of 'core' specialist language related to the subject area?
☐ Are learners equipped with skills and strategies which will allow them to operate effectively in English in the professional/occupational situation?
☐ Is there a balance between subject-specific language items (grammar, vocabulary, discourse structure) and operational skills and strategies in language use?
☐ Does the material consider the relationship between teachers and students? If so, is a collaborative approach encouraged?
☐ Is the material sufficiently flexible to meet the constraints often found in ESP work, eg by having a modular structure of non-sequential units?
☐ Can the material be used for individual study? If so, are learners given guidance on how to use the material in this way?
☐ To what extent do the learning activities mirror real-life situations, eg through task-based and skill-based activities?
☐ Do learning activities have outcomes or products which will help learners to evaluate their performance?

Chapter 12 Adapting published materials

1   Why adapt coursebooks?

I have suggested earlier that, despite the range and variety of published material on the market, it is rare to find a perfect fit between learner needs and course requirements on the one hand and what the coursebook contains on the other hand.

Every learning/teaching situation is unique and depends on factors such as these:

- the dynamics of the classroom
- the personalities involved
- the constraints imposed by syllabuses
- the availability of resources
- the expectations and motivation of the learners.

Material can nearly always be improved by being adapted to suit the particular situation where it is being used. This chapter considers when to adapt coursebooks and gives some suggestions on how to do it.

2   When to adapt

Adapting materials involves one or more of the following:

- leaving out some parts of the material
- adding material (published or your own)
- replacing material with something more suitable
- changing the published material to make it more suitable for your use.

We may need to adapt coursebooks because they are not ideal as they stand in any of the following areas:

- methods (eg an exercise may be too mechanical, lacking in meaning, too complicated)
- language content (eg there may be too much emphasis on grammar items that your students learn easily and not enough emphasis on those that they find difficult)
- subject matter (eg topics may not be interesting to the students or they may be outdated or not authentic enough)
- balance of skills (eg there may be too much emphasis on skills in the written language or on skills in the spoken language, or there may not be enough on integrating skills)
- progression and grading (the order of language items may need changing to fit an outside syllabus or the staging may need to be made steeper or shallower)

- cultural content (there may be some cultural references that need omitting or changing)
- image (a coursebook may project an unfriendly image through poor layout, low quality visuals, etc)

Teachers adapt coursebooks for all of the above reasons and in order to do so effectively we need to be sensitive to our students' interests, learning styles and motivation. We also need to be aware of what they find difficult and what they find easy, so as to be able to adapt materials in a way that makes them challenging linguistically and stimulating in their content, without being too difficult or user-unfriendly. In order to do this effectively, we need a good understanding of the nature of the materials that we are adapting, and experience of working in the learning/teaching situation which we are adapting the materials for. Given these requirements, materials adaptation can be a very worthwhile activity, giving added life and impact to even very ordinary coursebooks. There is a good deal of satisfaction in seeing an exercise or activity really take off and involve students because it was adapted to appeal to their interests and imagination.

The following diagram will help in deciding whether to adapt an exercise or other activity:

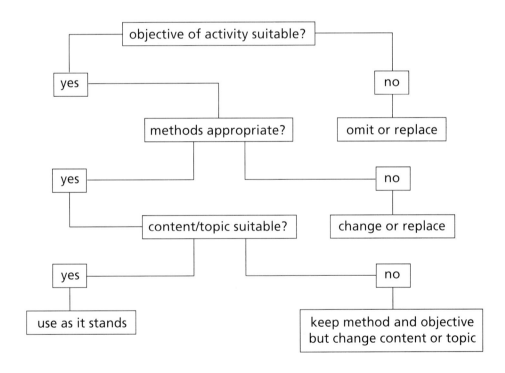

3   Supplementing and replacing material

Where material is lacking in a particular area or deals with the area in an unsuitable way, the options are to find supplementary material from other published sources or to produce your own material. Here we will look at supplementary material.

A coursebook may need supplementing in a number of different areas, but among the commonest are:

- reading
- listening
- pronunciation
- vocabulary
- grammar.

There are several sets of books which focus on **skills**, as we saw in Chapter 6, and these can be used as source material from which to select additional skills work. As they are graded according to level, it will be relatively straightforward to match the level of the supplementary material to the level of the learners and the coursebook. An advantage of using this kind of graded material is that it is easy to find exercises at a lower or higher level than the regular coursebook being used. This will accommodate students with differing skills profiles who need either remedial work or more advanced work in a particular skills area.

There are still some general courses which do not cover **pronunciation** as thoroughly or systematically as is necessary. In this case supplementary pronunciation books can be used, such as *English Aloud 1* and *2* (Haycraft 1994), *Headway Intermediate Pronunciation* (Cunningham and Bowler 1990), *Ship or Sheep?* (Baker 1981), *Tree or Three?* (Baker 1982) or *Elements of Pronunciation* (Mortimer 1985), all of which deal with aspects of pronunciation at different levels and with accompanying cassettes.

Vocabulary is covered more fully in modern coursebooks than was formerly the case, but there is still often scope for using supplementary vocabulary learning materials. These can be linked in with topic areas which come up in the main coursebook, and learners can have the opportunity to widen their vocabulary in connection with topics which interest them. There is a good deal of flexibility possible here, as learners can choose, either individually or in groups, which areas of additional vocabulary to focus on. Books such as *The Heinemann English Wordbuilder* (Wellman 1992) and *Wordpower* (Cunningsworth and Ferst 1982) are useful sources of supplementary material for vocabulary. It is important to check the level of the material and match it to your students' level, but material of a higher level can often be used when the focus is on vocabulary, because vocabulary does not necessarily get more difficult, it simply increases in quantity!

Most coursebooks cover **grammar** thoroughly, but there will still be plenty of occasions when additional grammar work is needed, or an alternative approach is required. Where the main coursebook uses an inductive approach to teaching grammar (the learner works out the rule from examples), many students will benefit from additional material that gives explanations and rules in straightforward language together with practice exercises on each grammar point. A good example of this type of material is *English Grammar in Use* (Murphy 1994).

It is worth noting however that the exercises in grammar books are usually made up of isolated sentences, which are useful for practising grammar and are appropriate for this kind of book. But they are not models of communicative language learning and are not sufficient on their own to equip learners to communicate. For this reason grammar books and most other supplementary materials are best used in conjunction with communicative coursebooks and not on their own.

4 A new role for the coursebook: inspiration and creativity

When evaluating a coursebook we look for its strengths and weaknesses and for how well it matches our requirements. We can also explore how far it lends itself to adaptation and if it offers possibilities of further development. Many coursebooks contain a lot of good ideas for teaching, but the actual examples contained in the book may not be quite right for a particular class.

The coursebook can then take on a new role, as an 'ideas bank', a source of practical examples of ideas for teaching and an inspiration stimulating teachers' creative potential. The benefits of such a partnership between coursebook and teacher are considerable: the coursebook is not expected to do what it manifestly cannot do, which is to tailor the material to each individual class, and teachers can base the development of their own materials on ideas from the book. This will help teachers to work in a more personal and creative way, with confidence and originality.

It is quite common, when searching through coursebooks for suitable materials, to come across exercises which at first glance seem unsuitable for use but which are based on sound ideas and are only inappropriate to a particular teaching situation because of their subject matter or style. A positive approach to published materials involves looking below the surface for underlying ideas that are good and can be developed further. If the basic idea is good, it can probably be used with different subject matter, with different contextualization or with a different skills focus.

The following examples are intended to illustrate how materials can be adapted, but are not held up as definitive models. They are included in the hope that they will spark the enthusiasm of readers to use their own creative talents in adapting their coursebooks when they feel it to be necessary.

5 Some examples of adapting materials

Personalizing drills to make them more relevant

This example comes from *New Guided English* Book 1 (Howe 1984), a coursebook for secondary schools in Malaysia, but similar drills could be found in countless books used around the world.

C. (Oral) Give replies like the ones in red:

> Do you have to clean the blackboard today?
> Yes, I have to clean it today. I will have to clean it tomorrow, too.
>
> Do you have to see the doctor today?
> Yes, I have to see him today and I will have to see him tomorrow, too.

1. Do you have to sweep the floor today?
2. Do you have to see the dentist today?
3. Do you have to help your father today?
4. Do you have to feed the dog today?
5. Do you have to look after your small brother today?
6. Do you have to look after the shop today?
7. Do you have to bathe your dog today?
8. Do you have to water the flowers today?
9. Do you have to cook the food today?
10. Do you have to do your homework today?
11. Do you have to clean your bicycle today?
12. Do you have to clean the window today?
13. Do you have to wear that tie today?
14. Do you have to help your mother today?

From *New Guided English*, Howe (Penerbit Fajar Bakti 1984)

The aim is to focus on *obligation* and teach *to have to (do something)*. The drill is straightforward and gives adequate practice in the mechanics of using *to have to* with present and future reference. The style is rather formal and such extensive and repetitive use of *have to* is improbable in informal speech, but the objective of the drill is to practise the structure rather than to relate it to a context of use. There is no situation given and the scene is not set. Nor do we know who the people are who are speaking. They are not identified, so there is no possibility of anything communicative taking place as the drill is rehearsed in class. It is clearly a mechanical, pre-communicative activity, and, so long as we realize this, it provides useful material.

Taking the drill as a starting point, we can develop the idea behind it and make the interaction more real and communicative by personalizing the content, whilst keeping the focus on the structure. This is one way of doing it:

- Ask the class about tasks that they do regularly, and write them on the board as a list.
- Ask the class to divide the list into things that they like doing and things that they don't like doing (this could be done as a group activity or as a whole class activity).
- Focus on the list of unpleasant tasks and give some examples using *have to* in the present and future *(will)* forms in the affirmative and interrogative.
- Students then work in pairs or small groups asking and answering questions *Do you have to ... today?* and *Will you have to ... tomorrow?*
- Introduce sentence *I always have to* and give examples.
- Students extend their responses to include this (which is a more natural use of *have to*): eg *I have to do my homework today and I'll have to do my homework tomorrow. I always have to do my homework.*
- If students are able, develop into more complex sentences, such as *I always have to finish my homework before I'm allowed to watch TV/go out with my friends.*

The important points are that students are talking about their own experiences in real life, and are communicating with one another through English, whilst at the same time focusing on using a particular structure.

Using authentic content

Authentic content is not to be confused with *authentic material*. Authentic content is using real facts and information instead of made-up content. The language used for this authentic content may itself be authentic, semi-authentic (simplified) or specially written, depending on the level. The attractively presented reading passage reproduced on pp 142–3 comes from *Fast Forward 2* (Black *et al* 1987) and gives information about a mythical island in the Indian Ocean.

66   Review unit three

 **B**

KELAPIA – PROFILE OF A DEVELOPING COUNTRY

1   Study the map of Kelapia. What resources does it possess?

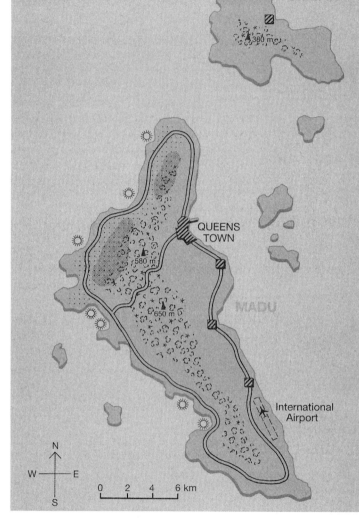

Forested land home of many rare birds, animals and plants

Plantations

Iron ore deposits (as yet undeveloped)

☼ Tourist developments

═══ Roads

▨ Towns

▲ Mountains

2   Work in groups of five. Each person in the group should read one of the pieces on Kelapia on the next page and then share the information to answer these five questions.

1   Where is Kelapia located?
2   What happened within a year of Kelapia gaining independence?
3   Which ethnic groups live on Kelapia?
4   What is the predominant religion of the country?
5   What was the traditional pattern of agriculture?

GEOGRAPHY

Kelapia is a small, island republic located roughly 900 miles off the coast of Africa in the Indian Ocean. It consists of two main islands, Madu and Tumbak and over 100 scattered islets, most of which are uninhabited. The archipelago lies totally within the tropics and has a monsoon climate. The total land area is 285 square kilometres, Madu (196 sq.km.), Tumbak 53 sq.km.). The main island, home of over 90% of the population, has many fine beaches, small stretches of coastal lowland used for agriculture and a mountainous and densely forested central ridge. There is plenty of fresh water on Madu though water becomes scarce on Tumbak during the dry season and there is very little ground water on any of the remaining islands.

HISTORY

Kelapia was first colonized by the French in the 18th century and ceded to the British in 1814. Plantations were established and labourers brought in from mainland African territories and the Indian subcontinent. Kelapia was granted its independence from Britain in 1979. Free elections were held and a progressive pro-western government was returned. However, within a year a military coup took place, reflecting deep-seated instability within the political system. The new government claims to be socialist and has the support of the Soviet Union, though it has yet to implement any far-reaching policy changes due to the strong colonial economic legacy.

ETHNIC COMPOSITION

The islanders are ethnically very mixed. The indigenous inhabitants, known as Kelawi, have intermarried to a certain extent but still preserve a distinct culture and ethnic identity. Later arrivals to the islands include a large number of East Africans and a smaller number of Indians from the Bombay area. Finally there is a small residual population of British and other European settlers.

Population by Ethnic Composition (%)
Kelawi	35%
African	40%
Indian	15%
Mixed	8%
Others	2%

RELIGION

Kelapia recognizes the right of the individual to practise any religion, as long as it does not conflict with the constitution and national interests. The majority of the Kelawi and Africans were missionized during the colonial period though the Indians have on the whole retained Hinduism as their faith. Both Kelawi and Africans mix Christianity and animism in their practices.

Population by Religion (%)
Protestant	65%
Catholic	23%
Hindu	10%
Muslim	2%

ECONOMY

The traditional base of the economy was, for over a century, plantation agriculture, relying on the export of copra and coconut products, cinnamon and vanilla. However, during the early 1960s the productivity of the coconut plantations declined due to the age of many of the palms and poor management of the estates, while the world market price of vanilla slumped drastically. Even though the value of cinnamon rose sharply during the same period, the government was forced to consider alternative sources of revenue.

From *Fast Forward 2*, Black *et al* (OUP 1987)

The activities involved in the reading passage on pp 142–3 include simple map-reading, a modified jigsaw reading and (on later pages not reproduced here) interpreting statistics, discussion and simulation. They form a very well designed package of activities, with plenty of skills work and student interaction within and between groups.

The subject of all this useful language work, however, is a non-existent country which, as such, is unlikely to be of interest to anyone, although students with good geographical knowledge of the area may recognize it as the Seychelles under a thin disguise!

The ideas and the activities are very good, so why not use them with some authentic content which will be interesting to the students and provide the opportunity to learn something about the world through English? In this way students' motivation is increased, the artificial barriers between subject areas are reduced and the value of English is enhanced through showing how it can give access to information and knowledge.

Using the framework of the coursebook activity, one way of adapting the material is this:

- Collect information about one or more countries that are in the news, or that are of interest for some other reason (eg near to students' home countries). Information can be obtained from different sources: tourist offices, embassies, encyclopaedias, the press, etc.
- Produce a simple map of the country, drawing one if necessary, based on the information obtained, and give a key to the symbols used.
- Select short pieces of text on about five different aspects of the country and give each a heading.
- Simplify text if necessary, but keep the original discourse structure as far as possible.
- Prepare introduction for setting the scene, using visuals if possible.
- Set questions on map and different sections of text for students to work on in groups using jigsaw technique.
- Collect statistics and set questions on the statistics.
- Design discussion and simulation where different interest groups in the country (eg farmers, factory workers, environmentalists) discuss strategies for the future development of the country.

Similar procedures could be used to exploit other kinds of genuine information, for instance a local issue such as road-building and environmental protection or social issues such as human rights. The important thing is to learn what students are interested in and build on that, showing that the English lesson is not just about English but is about all aspects of life.

Making dialogues communicative

Dialogue work is a necessary part of language learning and helps to develop a degree of fluency, particularly in the semi-automatic aspects of language use such as routine exchanges. However, because they are preordained, coursebook dialogues lack the unpredictability which is inherent in practically every authentic interaction. Even 'open dialogues' like the example on p 145 from *Kernel One* (O'Neill 1979) are essentially fixed dialogues, which have been gapped.

4

? **Open** ◦◦◦

dialogue

Mike Sutton and Anna Parker are talking.

MIKE: Let's ___ ___ the cinema.
ANNA: What ___ ___ ___ to see?
MIKE: "Blood and ___ ___"
ANNA: No, I don't ___ ___ films!
MIKE: Well what ___ "A Star ___ ___ ___"?
ANNA: ___ in it?
MIKE: Barbara ___
ANNA: And where's it ___?
MIKE: ___ the ABC.
ANNA: All right. ___ ___ see ___. When ___ ___ ___?
MIKE: At eight ten. ,

From *Kernel One*, O'Neill (Longman 1979)

A test which generally identifies fixed dialogues is to go through them line by line, masking off the lines that follow. If the 'correct' response to a question can only be worked out by looking at the masked-off lines below, then the dialogue is fixed and students are really being asked to reproduce, using clues and guesswork, what someone else has written, rather than creating their own dialogue.

The dialogue from *Kernel One* is a good example of this. The participants in the dialogue are told what to say, and more or less how to say it, giving them little freedom for self expression. Equally importantly, at certain points it is necessary to look at the answer before formulating the question – exactly the reverse of what happens in reality. In line 6 Anna is supposed to say *Who's in it?*, but she could equally well have said *What's in it?* It's only Mike's reply, *Barbara _____*, that tells us which is 'correct'.

Students need the sort of practice provided by fixed dialogues, but they also need to progress to less predictable models of interaction if they are to function in English independently. One stage in achieving this independence is to use *cue cards*, which can be easily made, based on coursebook dialogues. They are not wholly communicative, but rather a halfway stage between fixed and completely free dialogues.

The 'open dialogue' on p 146, again from *Kernel One*, allows the student, referred to as 'you', to initiate the conversation. But the conversation cannot begin until the student has seen the second line, which contains the answer. If the student knows the answer then there is no point in asking the question!

3 **Open dialogue**

You are asking Frank questions

1. YOU: ___ ___ ___ ___
   FRANK: Me? In Manchester.

2. YOU: ___ ___ ___ ___ ___, too?
   FRANK: Yes, they were.

3. YOU: ___ ___ ___ ___ ___?
   FRANK: At school? Well, I wasn't very good and I wasn't very bad, either.

4. YOU: ___ ___ ___ first job?
   FRANK: My first job? In a supermarket in Manchester.

5. YOU: How old ___ ___ when you ___ to London?
   FRANK: I was 18. I'm 20 now. But tell me something now! Why are you asking all these questions?

From *Kernel One*, O'Neill (Longman 1979)

Turning this dialogue into a pair of cue cards is very simple:

- Get pieces of plain card approximately 12 cm x 8 cm.
- Change each turn in the dialogue into an instruction written in English at a level that students can understand.
- Write the instructions for Student A on one card in the correct order, numbering them.
- Do the same for Student B.
- Colour code the cards (eg A cards have a red line across the top and B cards a blue line).
- Make sure that students have practised the same kind of dialogue in a more fixed form and that they understand how to use the cue cards.

A pair of cards developed from the open dialogue above would look like this:

Student A	**Student B**
You are talking to someone that you don't know very well. Begin the conversation with a question.	Someone that you don't know very well asks you some questions.
1. Ask him/her where he/she was born.	1. Answer the question.
2. Ask if his/her parents were born there too.	2. Answer the question.
3. Ask if he/she was good at school.	3. Answer the question. Ask if he/she is a student or has a job.
4. Respond (tell the truth!)	

Each student is being given a set of instructions which will interlock with a corresponding sequence on the partner's card. Each student must respond in real time as he/she cannot know in advance what the next move will be. In this way cue cards replicate some of the unpredictability of real conversation and prepare students for it.

Cue cards need not be based only on question and answer sequences but could reflect other types of conversation and dialogue such as agreement and disagreement, attempts at persuasion, etc.

6   Adapting outdated coursebooks

Teachers and students around the world often find themselves having to use coursebooks which are old and outdated in content. But some of these coursebooks contain sound ideas for teaching which are hidden beneath dull presentation or out-of-date topics.

Many of these ideas can be exploited if the presentation is improved and the content is brought up to date. Here is an exercise taken from *Guided Composition Exercises* (Spencer 1967), which, although old and out of print, is a veritable goldmine of good ideas for teaching writing skills at sentence and paragraph level. The aim of this exercise is to select a number of verbs from a range of alternatives, partly on the basis of style (eg *climbed* not *ascended* the wall), partly according to what are acceptable collocations (eg *picked* but not *plucked* the apples) and partly by recognizing what is normal or logical in behaviour (eg he *ran* home, he didn't *march* or *limp*). The exercise teaches (and tests) the learner's ability to use appropriate vocabulary items, selected according to different criteria.

148

Write the following passage out again, adding, in the spaces indicated by numbers, one verb from the lists with the corresponding numbers given below the passage. In each group of three verbs one is more appropriate in the context than the other two:

The boy (1) the wall to (2) the apples. He (3) half-a-dozen and (4) them in his pockets. As he was (5) down again he slipped and (6). The fruit in his pockets was squashed. He did not (7) himself, but he could not (8) the apples either. He (9) home and (10) his coat pockets.

  (1) climbed, leapt, ascended
  (2) discover, reach, inspect
  (3) plucked, seized, picked
  (4) hid, put, laid
  (5) jumping, slipping, falling
  (6) slid, collapsed, fell
  (7) wound, hurt, cut
  (8) eat, taste, use
  (9) marched, limped, ran
 (10) cleaned, washed, changed

From *Guided Composition Exercises*, Spencer (Longman 1967)

Some of the choices are fairly sophisticated and require considerable insight into the use of vocabulary. In contrast, the subject matter of the exercise is trivial and inconsequential, and the presentation outmoded.

The idea underlying the exercise is good and can still be exploited in today's context:

- Select a topical newspaper or magazine article at the right level of difficulty for your class.
- Choose vocabulary items that you want to explore further with the students for their style, collocations, etc.
- Delete these words, creating a gapped text.
- Give the original and alternative vocabulary items (as in the exercise that we have just looked at).
- Divide the class into groups of three or four students.
- Present the activity along these lines: 'Imagine that you are a group of sub-editors in a newspaper office and that an article has just been sent in by a junior reporter who is very indecisive. Sometimes he just can't make up his mind which words to use. Discuss the alternatives offered and agree on the best word to use in each case. Give your reasons.'
- Each group in the class can work on the same text and when they have finished they compare and discuss their choices. A 'best version' text is built up on the board by the whole class. Or different groups can do different texts and explain to the rest of the class why they chose the words they did.

Appendix Specifying aims and analysing the learning/teaching situation

When we are evaluating coursebooks for their suitability in particular situations, we need to build up a picture of the teaching situation in question, so that the material can be matched against it to see if there is a reasonable fit.

The following are some questions that you could ask about your own classes and school in order to help with this analysis.

Aims and objectives

- ☐ What are the aims of the English programme?
- ☐ Note any specific objectives, eg in terms of language items, functions, topics, skills, etc.
- ☐ Is there a detailed syllabus? If so, what does it consist of? In what terms is it expressed (grammar, functions, topics, skills, etc)?
- ☐ Are there prescribed or recommended coursebooks for use in class?
- ☐ If coursebooks are recommended, are they easy to change, if considered desirable by the teacher or school?
- ☐ Is the achievement of aims and objectives measured in any way, eg by periodic tests or end-of-course examinations? If so which aspects of English do the examinations focus on? What methods are used for testing, eg multiple choice, oral tests?
- ☐ Are there any very specific or unusual objectives that need to be taken into account?

The learning/teaching situation

- ☐ What is the status and role of English in the learners' home countries?
- ☐ What are their main purposes for learning English? How intensive is the programme? How much time per week is available for learning English?
- ☐ What resources are available in the school/college in terms of materials and equipment?
- ☐ What is the size of the classes/groups?
- ☐ Are the classes/groups homogeneous in level, ability, age, etc?
- ☐ What are the predominant values of the educational system (eg emphasis on knowledge/understanding/practical skills; emphasis on individual development of students or preparation for a place in society)?

The learners

- ☐ How old are the learners?
- ☐ What is their level of English?
- ☐ What previous learning experience have they had in English or other foreign languages?
- ☐ What expectations do learners have concerning the way they are taught?
- ☐ What are their preferred learning styles?
- ☐ What are the attitudes and motivation of the learners?
- ☐ What are their interests?

The teachers

- ☐ What is the accepted role of teachers in the educational system?
- ☐ How proficient in English are the teachers (if not native speakers)?
- ☐ How good an understanding of the structure of English do the teachers have?
- ☐ What methodological approach do teachers usually adopt?
- ☐ How free are teachers to vary the content and methods of their teaching?
- ☐ Do teachers normally demonstrate a high/low level of personal initiative?
- ☐ Do teachers have the right to adapt or supplement teaching material to suit their particular students? If so do they have the time and expertise to do so when necessary?

Not all of these questions will apply to every situation, but the answers that you get to some or all of them will help to build up a picture of your teaching situation which you can supplement with any other information that you have, and by your 'feel' for your students as individuals and as a group.

References

Abbs, B. and Freebairn, I. 1986 *Discoveries 2* (Longman)

Abbs, B. and Freebairn, I. 1989 *Blueprint Intermediate* (Longman)

Abbs, B. and Freebairn, I. 1990 *Blueprint One* (Longman)

Baker, A. 1981 *Ship or Sheep?* (CUP)

Baker, A. 1982 *Tree or Three?* (CUP)

Bell, J. and Gower, R. 1991 *Intermediate Matters* (Longman)

Bell, J. and Gower, R. 1992 *Upper Intermediate Matters* (Longman)

Black, V. *et al* 1987 *Fast Forward 2* (OUP)

Coleman, H. 1985 Evaluating teachers' guides: do teachers' guides guide teachers? In Alderson J. (ed.) *Lancaster Practical Papers in English Language Education, vol. 6: Evaluation* (OUP)

Cunningham, S. and Bowler, B. 1990 *Headway Intermediate Pronunciation* (OUP)

Cunningsworth, A. and Ferst, P. 1992 *Wordpower* (Macmillan)

Deller, S. and Jones, R. 1992 *Vista* (Heinemann)

Ferreira, L. 1981 *Notion by Notion* (Newbury House)

Forman, D. *et al* 1990 *Campus English* (Macmillan)

Garton-Sprenger, J. and Greenall, S. 1991 *Flying Colours* (Heinemann)

Geddes, M., Sturtridge, G. and Been, S. 1991 *Advanced Conversation* (Macmillan)

Geddes, M. and Sturtridge, G. 1992 *Elementary Conversation* (Macmillan)

Greenow, M. 1990 *Relay 3* (Nelson)

Haycraft, B. 1994 *English Aloud 1* and *2* (Heinemann)

Henrichsen, L. E. 1983 Teacher preparation needs in TESOL. In *RELC Journal* 14/1.

Hindmarsh, R. 1980 *Cambridge English Lexicon* (CUP)

Howe, D. 1984 *New Guided English* Book One (Penerbit Fajar Bakti Sdn. Bhd, Petaling Jaya)

Hymes, D. H. 1971 On communicative competence. In Pride, J. B. and Holmes, J. (ed.) 1972 *Sociolinguistics* (Penguin)

Jones, L. 1991 *Cambridge Advanced English* (CUP)

Leech, G. 1983 *Principles of Pragmatics* (Longman)

Levinson, S. 1983 *Pragmatics* (CUP)

Littlejohn, A. and Windeatt, S. 1989 Beyond language learning: perspectives on materials design. In Johnson, R. *The Second Language Curriculum* (CUP)

Littlewood, W. 1981 *Communicative Language Teaching* (CUP)

Lonergan, J. and Gordon, K. 1986 *New Dimensions 1* (Macmillan)

Macmillan 1991 *Macmillan Dossiers*

Mills, M. 1990 *Nexus* (Heinemann)

Mohamed, S. and Acklam, R. 1992 *The Beginners' Choice* (Longman)

Molteno Project 1987 *Bridge Plus One Teacher's Manual* (De Jager-Haum)

Mortimer, C. 1985 *Elements of Pronunciation* (CUP)

Murphy, R. 1994 *English Grammar in Use* new edition (CUP)

O'Neill, R. 1979 *Kernel One* (Longman)

O'Neill, R. and Mugglestone, P. 1989 *Third Dimension* (Longman)

Phillips, D. and Sheerin, S. 1990 *Signature Elementary* (Nelson)

Potter, M. 1989 *English Around You* (Macmillan)

Potter, M. 1991 *International Issues* (Macmillan)

Revell, J. 1990 *Connect* (Macmillan)

Richards, J. and Rodgers, T. 1986 *Approaches and Methods in Language Teaching* (CUP)

Risager, K. 1990 Cultural references in European textbooks: an evaluation of recent tendencies. In Buttjes, D. and Byram, M. *Mediating Languages and Cultures* (Multilingual Matters)

Rodriguez, M. and Barbisan, C. 1992 *Freewheeling 2* (Heinemann)

Sajvaara, K. and Lehtonen, J. 1978 quoted in Kramsch, C. 1981 *Discourse Analysis and Second Language Teaching* (Center for Applied Linguistics, Washington, DC)

Scotton, C. and Bernsten, J. 1988 Natural conversations as a model for textbook dialogue. In *Applied Linguistics* 9/4: 372–84

Shepherd, J. and Cox, F. 1991 *The Sourcebook Pre-intermediate* (Longman)

Shepherd, J., Hopkins, A. and Potter, J. 1992 *The Sourcebook Intermediate* (Longman)

Soars, J. and L. 1986 *Headway Intermediate* (OUP)

Spencer, D. 1967 *Guided Composition Exercises* (Longman)

Swan, M. and Walter, C. 1990 *The New Cambridge English Course* (CUP)

Vince, M. 1992 *Highlight Upper Intermediate* (Heinemann)

Viney, P. and K. 1990 *Grapevine 1* (OUP)

Ward, A. and Lonergan, J. 1988 *New Dimensions 3* (Macmillan)

Wellman, G. 1992 *The Heinemann English Wordbuilder* (Heinemann)

White, R. 1988 *The ELT Curriculum* (Blackwell)

White, R. and Williams, E. 1989 *Formula One* (Macmillan)

Widdowson, H. 1978 *Teaching Language as Communication* (OUP)

Widdowson, H. 1979 *Explorations in Applied Linguistics* (OUP)

Wilkins, D. 1976 *Notional Syllabuses* (OUP)

Index